DOMINIC BOAG

THE BOY NEXT DOOR WITH
THE INCREDIBLE GIFT

THE VOICE OF SPIRIT

This edition first published in paperback by
Michael Terence Publishing in 2023
www.mtp.agency

ISBN 9781800945661

Cover image
Dominic Boag

Foreword

I have been privileged to observe many mediums during my life. Sometimes they were involved in activities and experiments at the Scottish Society for Psychical Research (SSPR). At other times, I sought them out to help guide and heal others – even dealing with the occasional haunting. And I have consulted mediums privately, for the gifts only they can offer. While I have always appreciated the effort made by mediums and psychics, I have often been left disappointed.

Yet, there are those transformative moments, when authentic spiritual gifts are demonstrated, abilities most of us can only imagine. We realise the immense power of Spirit to heal us, proving that our passed loved ones never really leave us. I've had my fair share of phenomenal experiences with Spirit, but nothing comes to what Dominic Boag has given me.

I have tested his ability and he has consistently impressed me with his clairaudient mediumship. I have seen first-hand his generous, caring and yet modest nature. He is filled with a genuine desire to help and heal those suffering from grief. For all the obstacles life has thrown at him, he has consistently devoted himself to serving others.

When you read his memoir, you'll understand the kind of medium, the kind of man, that Dominic is. Fair to say, he's had his grief and disappointments: let down by those who profess to know better, dark moments and great loss. Personally, I've found that the most valuable diamonds shine brightest against, and in spite of, these dark backgrounds.

Despite his rousing successes as a medium, Dominic credits Spirit for his gifts. However, I firmly believe that Dominic deserves your admiration too.

A natural teacher, Dominic is dedicated to sharing proof of life after death, that our loved ones continue to walk with and watch over us. And he does this with unfailing compassion and kindness. I commend Dominic and his book greatly. Readers should prepare themselves to take the first steps of their spiritual journey. You won't be able to think of life the same again. That is Dominic's true gift.

Nick Kyle
Former President of
The Scottish Society for Psychical Research (SSPR)

Why Write a Book?

Growing up as a young medium, I knew early on that I wanted to write a book, a book that would inspire other young people and other young mediums. I wanted to inspire them to have aspirations and make their dreams a reality. More importantly, I wanted to tell young developing mediums, 'Hey, you have a place in this world.'

When I first started developing my mediumship, Spiritualism and Spiritualist churches were not places for young people. Not due to any conscious exclusion, but speaking to the dead is not exactly what you'd call a young person's interest. The mediums at churches or on the telly were older women, wearing kaftans and crystal necklaces that would clang together. Or older men with greying, long hair, also wearing kaftans and crystal necklaces. I think I brought the average age at the Butterfly Centre down by a couple of decades.

I want to, I guess, prove to both the older established generation of mediums and the young developing generation that young people should be welcomed, they just need to be nurtured and taught. After all, I am proof of that.

Later in the book, I talk about what makes a good medium or a promising potential medium. Spoiler alert: one criterion I talk about is that those who have experienced loss and trauma can make good mediums. They have been touched by death and have the personal emotional experience to connect with people in grief. In the book, I wanted to talk about this, to show that trauma does not need to define your path. It might deepen your empathy for others and your appreciation and understanding of life. But it is what you do with that trauma, that pain and heartache, that is important.

At a young age, I lost two father figures. In my late teens, I was diagnosed with a condition that was slowly stealing my sight. I understand trauma. I know that I could have dealt with it differently and that I could have let it define me. My life would be very different if I had chosen to focus on everything that I had lost, everything that I didn't have. But, instead, I rose from it. It is part of my life and led me to where I am, but it is not my entire life. In writing this book, I wanted to help people, especially young people, to understand this. That I see and know and understand your hurt, but don't let that be all you are.

I want to show that being young and inexperienced shouldn't hinder you from exploring your spirituality. I want to show that your life doesn't have to centre around your trauma; you can grow from it. I also wanted to illustrate that being disabled does not need to stop you either. The world is not built for disabled people. Alterations and allowances can be made, but daily life can be restricted, whether you're in a wheelchair, suffer from a degenerative disease, or are visually impaired like me.

When I began losing my sight, I didn't know what would happen to me or what I would be able to do with my life. My dreams of writing a book were truly over, I thought. Even when beginning as a medium, I didn't know how I would conduct readings or shows without my sight. But I found a way. I don't think I managed this in spite of my disability, but because of it. It was a hurdle I needed and learnt to jump over. If you come to see me at a show, I will tell audience members that they're going to need to shout out to claim a message. And my medium skills have not suffered. They grew and Spirit helped me to develop my clairaudience.

Being disabled does not need to dis-able your life. It does not need to stop you from living the life that you want or, quite frankly, deserve. I have found a way to live with the obstacles of my disability. It is hard, yes, but I have not and will not let it stop me. I am disabled, I am registered blind. I am also a medium who has written a book and travels the world. If I can do it, I hope everyone feels that they can too.

When I was young, there was no book or story to tell me that it was going to be okay, that I was going to be okay, and that despite everything, my life can still be what I want it to be. This book is about my aspirations and my want to inspire; but I also feel a level of responsibility, to tell the story that would have inspired me, and made a difference in my life. Just as I pass on my spiritual lessons during classes and workshops, I want to pass on my message of hope and strength. If only one person reads this and finds hope and courage, becomes motivated to explore their aspirations, or finds a way through their trauma or disability, it will be a job well done.

1

First the hairs on my neck stood on end, the room statically charged. The temperature dropped, suddenly cold, and I could feel, sense, a presence behind me, waiting. Despite the slight glow about this outline, like rays of sun behind a cloud, Dad stood before me, solid and real, just as he had done when he was alive. I should have been afraid if it were not for the feeling of love that emanated from him.

Softly he spoke, almost like a whisper, telling me, reminding me that he would always be with us, and he was sorry he had to leave, but he was okay. He charged me with looking after the family now. Just as my emotions were catching up with my sight, he began to fade, disappearing into a single point of light.

If you had asked me then, in that moment, if Dad was still with us, I would have been convinced he was. For a dream-like moment, he had not passed at all. But even as the room shifted back to how it was, I realised then I had seen his spirit – that he was in fact gone.

***

There is a poetry to it really, a psychic medium born on a Friday 13th, no date more associated with superstition and the spirit world. Perhaps it was destined for me to work with Spirit, even from that day in 1991, when I, a stroke of good luck, was born.

My parents' relationship was a troubled one, my father's alcoholism preventing him from holding down a full-time job and making him to be abusive. He would come and go from the house, sometimes disappearing for days at a time. Whenever he did come back, he was drunk and foul. On more than one occasion, my sister Danielle and I would hide in a wardrobe, hearing my father returning from the pub, fearing a beating.

After a particular severe beating when I was five years old, my mother couldn't take it anymore. We left in 1996.

Nothing was lost in the separation: I did not miss him, love him nor took any pleasure in his company. The fact that he was my father was a mere biological fact. My only reminder of this man was the bruises he left on my body. We never sought him out after we left.

In 2016, he passed away.

Surrounded by family, friends and good neighbours, my mother brought Danielle and me up in a flat overlooking the spectacular views of the Clyde. We were happy there. Without my father, my mother thrived as a strong, independent single parent – traits I hope to have inherited, along with her compassionate and loyal nature.

Along with my mother, my grandparents were a great and constant support, a closeness that has never waned. As well as a support, my grandparents are inspirations to me, influencing how I work and live – I have always tried to make my values match theirs. My grandfather Alec worked as the Head of the Children's Panel in Scotland, dealing with hearings involving children and young people. His compassion, his ability to work with people from all walks and stages of life and not judge, I carry with me, using it in my own line of work.

My desire to help and heal might have come from my grandfather, but my love of interacting with people, getting to know them through and aside from spirit communication, comes from my landlady granny. As she worked behind the bar, I'd be sat there, eating cherries and occasionally making mischief. When conducting readings or doing shows, I always like to bring in some comedic, almost land lady-like joviality. Just because I'm talking with the dead, doesn't mean the show has to be all doom and gloom.

As happy as we were, our lives improved even more when my mother met and fell in love with John. Danielle and I finally had a decent loving caring man in our lives. Whereas my father had been a shadow of the first few years of my life, John became a hero, rescuing all of us. From that first meeting at McDonalds where he stuck fries up his nose, pretending to be a walrus, to sneaking around while Mum was at the bingo to buy a pet dog, he was a family man through-and-through, the kind of man everyone knew or knew of.

It was John who taught me to fish, spending hours digging for worms in Coronation Park in Port Glasgow. And when we weren't catching fish, we were buying tropical ones, keeping them in a huge tank. Even if I didn't really know what to do when he kicked a football to me, I finally had the father-and-his-boy relationship that I had missed out on before.

After marrying Mum, he adopted us and we were all too happy to take his surname. In truth, he is only father I have ever known – the man who raised me and the one I call Dad. With the addition of my younger brother Stuart, our little family, through trial and tribulation and heartache, was complete.

Even as a young boy, I was labelled a 'chatter'; my mother remembers me as an early talker. From the 'Pink Group' in nursery, all the way through high school, I just could not help myself. There is always so much to learn from listening and talking to people, and those lessons have always meant more to me than dreary subjects like Maths and French.

Outside the classroom, I was able to put this chattiness to good use, from disruptive Achilles' heel to shining quality. I was part of my local drama group, involved with - or rather starring in - several educational videos, one on the dangers of drinking, and one of the effects and consequences of drug abuse. Covered by The Greenock Telegraph, I was labelled a 'real community hero' and spoke on behalf of other young people doing positive community-oriented work. My love of the chat and my wish to help and heal were gradually coming into their own.

Beyond acting and being a spokesperson, it was time to think about what I would do after school. For a year, I studied Hairdressing at James Watt College, where my efforts began to pay off – I was again surrounded by and interacting with a whole tapestry of different kinds of people. There was no one I wouldn't have a wee chinwag with. I only studied hairdressing for a year, before I was offered a better-paid role as a customer service advisor at Hero TSC call centre in Greenock. I would be talking even more.

At home, history was repeating itself. Similar to my biological father, my dad had his demons when it came to alcohol. By now, we all knew the drill – he would come and go as he pleased, leaving for days at time to find his fix, reappearing only when Mum was ready to forgive him. After the warmth, love and father figure that Dad had provided, it was a blow to watch him follow the same path as my father, choosing drink over his family. Old wounds were reopened; old pains and fears were remembered.

Unfortunately, I couldn't talk my way out of tragedy. In 2006, Dad passed away from alcohol-related issues. Like my father before, Dad disappeared and did not return. But unlike my father's death, Dad's passing was crushing, and I began to experience my first bitter taste of loss, and at such a critical point in my life. Yes, I had the consolation of my family and friends like Siobhan - who I had clicked with from the beginning and stayed with while I grieved - but life had already changed. A man who I had chosen to call Dad, whose surname I had taken, who had raised me, was gone.

Maybe his visitation was a final gift. It was through this loss that I began to feel and connect with the spirit world. Like most teenagers, I was on the computer at the time, again chatting away, when I felt the atmosphere in the room shift. Like the smell before a storm or the building of static in the air, I began to sense a presence before I saw him.

Dad stood before me – other than a soft glow around his body, like a halo or an aura, he was as I remembered him alive. And, for a second, I thought he was. From him emanated waves of love and I heard him speak, apologies he offered and tasks he gave me. It was my job now to look out for our family. Before I could muster a response, my emotions overpowering my speech, he had left again. The room changed again, as if nothing had ever happened. Had I fallen asleep? Had it been a dream? Had his death been a dream? No, even then, I knew what had happened was undeniable and unforgettable.

An incredible moment like that is indelible, the memory latched on to my soul. Dad had planted the first spiritual seeds that I would nurture and grow and tend throughout my life. But when you're 14, it's hard to think that far ahead. For as long as I could, I kept what happened that night to myself. Mum was still grieving the loss of her husband, my siblings their father; sharing what I had seen could only cause more sadness. I could not do that to my family. I stored it in the back of my mind and continued my life as ordinarily as possible.

What had happened to me, what the appearance of Dad's spirit has begun, could not be undone. The extraordinary and the spiritual was everywhere, left like breadcrumbs leading me to something, to somewhere. I would think about the most random people, like the father of my best friend Siobhan, and I'd bump into him, just around the corner. I became increasingly sensitive about people lying; I began to be aware of future events. Coincidences you might say, and I simply laughed it off with friends at first. Gradually, these moments happened more and more, bursts of intuition and premonitions, and still I never thought of myself or claimed to be psychic.

Even as more and more of these 'coincidences' happened, my intuition leading me to wherever I needed to be, I was still doubtful, couldn't firmly grasp what was happening to me. After all, I was a young boy who'd not long lost his dad; I was naïve to assume that I had been given some gift or ability. My imagination was running wild, fuelled by grief and loneliness.

And still Dad kept coming back. Time and time again, he returned, often with messages for Mum: messages that I could not possibly know and that I could not pass on. At least not yet.

It's different now, where these messages I give and connections I make are healing and powerful for those I read. When you're in the middle of mourning, when it's your own personal grief, it's hard to think of these messages as healing. But this is what Dad was trying to teach me all along; helping me appreciate that the power of my gift, to communicate the uncommunicable, is reassuring and heartening. I try and pass on the same warmth Dad gave me to everyone I read for.

One moment that sticks in my memory was being in Greenock Town Centre with my gran who had got chatting to a friend of hers. As I stood waiting, I saw a man with them and I couldn't understand why he was being ignored, my gran and her friend carrying on as if he wasn't there. When I tried to speak to him, he vanished. Had he been there at all? Ignored by my gran and then disappearing. Later, it emerged that the man had been the husband of Gran's friend, or rather his spirit.

Things continued to progress beyond premonitions and I began to see more and more spirits, people that others couldn't, like the spirit of Gran's friend's husband. They came unbidden and sometimes at the most peculiar or inconvenient of times. Deceased teachers at school would try and talk to me, knowing that I could see them. As much as I wish they could be more helpful, give up some test answers or something, more often than not these spirits would lead me into trouble. Talking again, the living teachers would say. It's hard to argue back when your excuse is that you're in the middle of talking to your teacher's dead relative. Again, I kept these interactions to myself. They would be unbelievable to most people, and I would be weird or crazy to them. To me, every moment, every interaction with a spirit, every glimpse of the future, was intriguing.

As if guided by fate or destiny, or maybe even Dad, Mum and Danielle visited a medium at The Butterfly Fellowship, a Spiritualist church in Port Glasgow. Now, up to this point, Mum and Danielle had no clue what I was getting up to, seeing spirits and having visions. So, when Dad came through and revealed all via the medium, they rushed home to ask me if this was true.

"Anything you want to tell us," Mum had said. All I could think of was the bottle of vodka hidden in my bedroom. "I've been told what you can do. Is it true?" There was no point denying it now. As soon as I started, it all came bubbling out of me. With the cat well and truly out the bag, I admitted that I had seen Dad and other spirits. I didn't claim to understand it all, but I explained everything I could, including why I had kept it secret for so long.

Anyone being told their child can speak to spirits is going to be a bit taken aback. The idea of being thought mad were still at the forefront of my mind. But Mum eased herself into it, and once she began to watch me work, to show her what I was capable of, there no fear or apprehension. Maybe it was no surprise to her at all. After all, as a child, I would sit on her knew and play with the crystal ball-shaped necklace she wore, already telling her that I could see her future.

The following week, I sat in the audience of that same Spiritualist church. The performing medium, Sandra McFadden – who also happened to be the president of the church – zoned in on me, told me that I could do what she was doing, that I could be a medium. Not only that, she was willing to teach me. Never one to hesitate and intrigued by the journey this gift could take me on, I attended her development class the next night.

While my school pals were going to football or swimming clubs, I was going to classes and services at a Spiritualist church, harnessing my gift and learning the ropes of mediumship three nights a week. At age 16, under Sandra's tutelage, I began to publicly demonstrate my skills as a medium.

Up on the stage, a setting I was already used to, I had nothing to lose. I stood there, not even thinking about that first time with Dad, and presented myself to Spirit. 'Here I am', I thought, and I put my entire trust in Spirit. As I started to connect, I became aware of a spirit stepping forward. I was able to identify this spirit as a man, a brother. I connected to a woman in the congregation. Accurate information, things I could never have possibly known, just spilled out of me. More and more it came, personal details that clearly resonated with the grieving sister. Overwhelmed by the breadth of information I gave, I began to get emotional too. My trust in Spirit had paid off.

What a powerful experience that first reading was. Not only to put all that training and my gift into practice, to speak of things received from Spirit, but to witness the emotional impact it could have. Through the tears and the answers, there was an instinct inside me, confirming that not only was this what I was meant to do, but that it would a source of healing to many.

Through the training that Sandra provided, I began to trust my intuition and listen to the spirits' voices, discerning them from my own internal chatter. This was not my imagination and I was not going crazy. People's responses to my readings were encouraging and helped my confidence grow; their belief in me helped me believe in myself. Still, I tried to keep my medium life separate from my ordinary teenager life, telling none of my school friends about my, let's say, unusual extra-curricular activities. How do you tell a bunch of teenagers that you're speaking to the dead without them thinking you've lost the plot?

As ever, my grandparents supported me, even if they were unsure about it. Ever practical, my gran couldn't see this becoming a career. As man of the house, she told me that I needed to get a 'proper' job, to pay the bills. Of course, she had my best interests at heart, but my life has led me down a very unusual path and one they have come to support. And while they attend my shows, seeing for themselves the audience I bring in, I will never read for them. Some things are best left unsaid.

Just as some parents sit with their children to help with homework, Mum helped and supported my mediumship. She would invite her friends over, friends who had been there through her grief, and now wanted to be there for me. They began to accept that what I had was certainly a gift. One evening, I was practicing, conducting a reading for Mum's pal Shelia. The spirit of her son made himself known, a son that none of us knew she had. Same as at the Spiritualist church, I began to reel off accurate information about her son and his life, reducing her to tears.

A healing effect followed Shelia's reading; she was comforted by the fact that her son was still alive, just in a different way. To this day, it is this healing effect that is at the core, the heart, of my work. Even now, Shelia reminds me of the evidence I was able to give her, the healing that I had offered and affected through my gift.

Sandra was keen to develop my skills further; she said she could see something special in me, more than just my gift. It was Sandra that pushed me, urged me to grow and step outside of my comfort zone. As my confidence grew, as my trust in Spirit and my abilities strengthened, I began to serve the church as a medium, later becoming the church's Vice President. From there, I guess word of my abilities began to spread, and people began to request private readings and I was inundated with messages from Spiritualist churches all over Scotland, asking for me to demonstrate.

I had had a taste of what I was capable of. I could present audiences and individuals with messages from their loved ones, supplying evidential proof that they were there, present with us, but unseen. The skills are one thing, but knowing how these skills could help and heal those in mourning, those who had lost people and were looking for answers, that spurred me on. Further I wanted to reach, help even more people. Doors began to open, close to home and internationally.

I was invited to represent Scotland at an Under 25s mediumship event at a conference organised by the International Spiritualist Federation. The invites and requests poured in: a real motivator and confidence boost. As I was ready to receive messages from spirits, and give all the healing messages I could, something changed again. With all I had received, I began to lose something else.

2

It would be a mistake to think that being a medium and having this connection to Spirit, would mean that I knew what I was going to do with my life. But at 17, I did not, who does? Mediumship was a hobby, a gift I could nurture and enjoy. It was a stage that I would surely outgrow. Maybe my interest would dim; maybe the voices would quieten and maybe I wouldn't be the only student checking out the paranormal and occult books from the school library. Anyway, it was never a career opportunity. Could you imagine going to your school's careers advisor and saying, 'I can talk to the dead, so I think being a professional medium might be an option? Thoughts?' But I had to live in the physical world and, in the physical world, I needed a job.

In the November of 2008, I began working at a call centre, a newly launched service as part of Sky UK. After all, it was an excuse to blether with people. I was still attending circles and the Spiritualist church, but my mediumship was tucked away at the back of my mind for now. However, sometimes there was no stopping it.

It is not as simple as an on-off switch with mediumship, but I tried to back away from Spirit when I was working. On platform, I'd be ready to go, calling on my dad to bring the spirits forward and allow them to approach me. Sometimes, though, spirits would insist on interacting with me: a spiritual nudge to get on with it.

Staring at a screen for hours a day, I easily found myself in a trance-like state. When I talked with customers, I sometimes tapped into their emotions. In those moments, spirits would make themselves known. I would hear snippets of voices, voices that weren't coming through my headset. I would be waiting for systems to load, making small talk with a customer, when I'd hear something and make a passing remark.

'That's my wife,' they would whisper to me, confirming the personal meaning behind passwords. 'I know you're missing him, but at least his cancer is gone.' I told one customer. The details would come intuitively.

Working at the call centre was merely a job and being a medium was a hobby. What I really aspired to was joining the police. As a wee boy, I was convinced that my grandfather was a policeman. He would regale me with the most outrageous stories, who he'd 'put away', flashing his 'warrant card' at me. Always my inspiration, of course, I wanted to follow him into the police force. It had all been in my imagination though, the fun and games between grandparent and grandchild. As an adult, it dawned on me that he had been way too short to be a policeman. So convincing had he been, his stories inspired by his real work on the Children's Panel. But this was my dream, and I was ready to apply for the Police Cadets.

While I am not a disciple of fate or destiny, I prefer the term 'divine timing', things do come and go, to and from you, when you need them. And it came to light that this was not the 'divine time' for me to be a police officer.

It was a typical day in the call centre, and something was just off. The screen wasn't clear, everything was watery like when you've rubbed your eyes. My vision just did not seem right. I messed with the computer settings, the brightness and the contrast but nothing changed. I put one hand over each eye and found my left eye was weak and my sight blurry. Mum made an appointment at the optician's; nothing to worry about, it was simply time for me to start wearing glasses.

For two and a half hours we were in the opticians. Not a single optician could tell exactly what was the matter, why my left eye was weak and it was no longer just needing glasses. Worrying words such as 'abnormality' and 'emergency referral' began to be bandied about. All I needed, all I wanted, was a pair of specs and a note for the police, confirming that my sight was fine.

Over a couple of days, whilst still working, I was shuffled between various doctors at the hospital. Still, they could not say anything conclusive or give a final word as to what was happening to me. A few weeks later, however, some concern began to creep in, when I noticed another change and my sight worsening again. Another change meant another appointment.

This time, the doctor wanted to admit me for a brain scan. I looked at Mum, she looked at the doctor. Some concern grew into a lot of worry in those seconds. The cogs in my mind began to turn. Brain scan must mean brain tumour; brain tumour must mean that this will continue; this means an operation, maybe several. This means I could lose all my sight and permanently. By the look on her face, Mum was thinking the same. And the doctor confirmed this, or at least that a brain tumour pressing on my optic nerve was suspected. At just 18 years old, I might have had a brain tumour and was sent away for a scan.

Lying down, ready for the scan, I had been given headphones to help keep me calm. Eyes squeezed closed, I was manoeuvred into the machine, worrying and wondering what the hell was going to happen to me next. As anyone who's had a brain scan will tell you, the noise that the machine makes is as terrifying as thinking what it will show. Disorienting, discomforting, and disturbing.

Between the scan and the results, I imagined myself dead several times over. What will the scan show? What will happen to me? Can a brain tumour explode? Can a brain tumour bleed? When Mum and I were finally called in for the results, the relief we felt to know that the MRI had come back clear was unbelievable. But the issues persisted and my sight grew weaker.

Another round of tests with another specialist, this time Dr Mansfield. During our initial appointment, he quizzed us on our family and our genetics, in case anything might have been passed down. Only during this meeting did I discover that my grandmother was adopted. I went for blood tests, I was given eye drops, and my eyes and sight were tested constantly. There is not an eye test in existence that I wasn't put through.

During this time, I was still going to the Spiritualist church but not as much as I had. Being 18, I was busy clubbing and socialising, exploring my new-found adult freedoms. Losing my sight, as a possibility or a fear, I'd never factored into my mediumship. Sure, when I work, I use visual cues: 'the woman in the blue jumper', 'the man with the green shirt', but I never thought this would go away somehow. Denial was my default setting: that I wasn't losing my sight, that I couldn't be going blind at 18 years old.

After the possible brain tumour scare, I was now trying to stay optimistic. I was 18 and healthy; I was not, could not be losing my sight. All I needed was a pair of glasses, which I had no qualms about. Mum had glasses, Danielle had glasses, and so did both my grandparents. All these tests, all this worry over some specs.

Yet, during another morning at work, all the fear and worry and terror about what was happening to me, still undiagnosed, came back with a bite. My sight, I could tell, had worsened. What had happened that first day to my left eye, was now happening to my right. I told my manager that I needed to go home, that I could barely see my computer screen. He didn't know what to do; no one did. Mum was called to collect me.

Waiting for Mum and sitting with another manager, I finally broke down. Everything around me was failing. Everything that I was – my positivity, my confidence – was being ripped away. Something sinister was going on, something that no one knew about and that no one could stop. As I sobbed and sobbed, my manager held me. In the backseat of Mum's car, curled up, I continued to sob.

By the time we got to the hospital, Dr Mansfield had the results of the latest test. Leber's Hereditary Optic Neuropathy they called it. Fancy words to dress up my realised fear – I was losing my sight. I was eventually going to go blind. Not since we had lost Dad had I seen Mum cry the way she did that day, embraced by the nurse who had seen me through all the tests.

This has to be wrong, I thought, the diagnosis has to be wrong. I refused to believe what Dr Mansfield was telling me. I would get better again. I would be able to see again. Okay, I might need glasses, maybe now, a year, a decade from now. I would not be blind, not until I had grey hair and wrinkles. But denials are not cures, and refusing a diagnosis is not listed as a recommended treatment, and still I fought against it.

To then go and share the news, share the grief and pain with the world, would mean acknowledging it. Telling my grandparents was hard, and they were distraught. Like Mum, Gran had always been the stronger one, a survivor, but all she could do was cry when we broke the news to her. It was not just grief and a shared pain she felt. We told her the full name of the condition, and she understood that she was part of the 'Hereditary' in Leber's Hereditary Optic Neuropathy. She wept with guilt, angry that she had not known, had let this happen to her grandchild.

'If I had known,' she said, 'I would not have had children.'

'But if you hadn't had children, we wouldn't have each other. We will get through this, together, as a family,' I struggled to say with my last ounce of courage. 'We always have. We always will.'

Somehow, I found the courage to face my family. I was the man of the house. I had no choice but to be encouraging, strong and brave for all of us. Together, we had suffered through abuse and loss and death and disappointment. We had built up resilience through the hardest of things any one person or any one family could experience. This was one more thing for us to fight through and come out the other side of.

What a wonderful story that was to tell everyone, to promise that I would be able to bounce back, that I was strong enough to handle this. But, alone in my bedroom, fighting and frightened of my diagnosis like a monster under the bed, the darkness and depression crept in. Taking time off work to deal with my condition, I spent hours just staring at the walls of my bedroom. In my head, I shouted, 'Why me?' Why on earth was this happening to me, to someone like me, someone of my age?

Somewhere down the road, after a heart-breaking and life-changing moment, we all question God, our very belief in God. If there is a God, how could He, why would He allow something so awful to happen? For me, having had Dad with me in Spirit, showing me this afterlife and supporting my gift, was a great source of comfort. Yet, when I needed him the most, he was nowhere to be found. I had been abandoned.

No signs or messages came through. No whispers in my ear, and no images popped into my head. The gift that I had thought I had been blessed with, the Spirit I had put my faith in, was failing me. At the Spiritualist Church, I had seen and known about spiritual healing, the peace that messages from departed loved ones could bring. Why was I being denied this help? Why me? Why God? Why *not* me? Further and further, I turned to the encroaching darkness of my depression, and away from the light of Spirit.

I was alone. I didn't know how to cope with Mum. Her constant maternal worry, her 'how are yous', and her 'what can I dos', were exhausting and, more often than not, went unanswered. I was embarrassed. I was weakened and less than by my sight now. When someone spoke, I couldn't look them in the eye. My confidence was knocked. My aspiration to join the Police was well and truly over.

I became disconnected from my friends, those who didn't know how to approach or 'deal' with me anymore. Having a medium for a friend is one thing, but having to help a friend with depression was another obstacle, another complication to negotiate. Many just didn't know what to do. Only friends like Siobhan, who'd been with me from the beginning, who'd been there when we got the results, inspired and encouraged me. She reached out her hand to me and helped me begin the ascent out of the hole I was in.

Like a prisoner, I slowly allowed myself to be reintroduced to society, to step out from my room and its darkness, into the lightness and hope of the outside world. Shafts of light began to break through. Yes, there were those moments when the light would dim again and the darkness seemed to grow darker. But this was the beginning.

During this time, when I began to make small steps outside the four walls of my bedroom, my gift began to awaken again. Instead of seeing spirits gathering around me, I began to hear the most beautiful but subtle voices, their soothing words whispering in my ear. Their words brought reassurance, 'Trust us. Believe in us. We're here with you.' Becoming aware of spirits' presence again, not by sight, but by instinct and intuition and the prickling sensation on my skin, encouraged me to return to the church. Another shaft of light broke through my darkness.

With my ears tuned into Spirit and my faith in my gift slowly being mended, there was one person I was waiting to hear from again. I started to ask where Dad was, where he had been through this most difficult time, and why he had not been with me. Not until we held a physical séance, did I get my answers. Through the work of fellow medium, Scott, Dad spoke to me again. As much as I had been hurting, Dad was hurting equally. As a parent, he explained, it was too hard for him to watch me in my darkest moments, to not be able to do anything or help. He explained that I had to pull though, even while his helplessness pulled him away.

Mum could ask me question after question, pester me and do practical things like cook and clean for me. Dad was stuck, unable to comfort or assist from the spirit world. I understood then why I couldn't hear or see him, why I'd been left rather than abandoned to find my own strength to break through.

As I began to feel lighter again, adjusting to this new life and new mediumship, the outside world continued moving forward. While I had been sitting in my room, Dr Mansfield worked to help me. Checking and approving my liver and kidney function, I was given big intimidating boxes of drugs, tablets that I had to take three times every day. The side effects were the first thing I felt: the cramps in my legs in the middle of the night, the newly-sprouted chest hair. Ultimately it was the only thing I felt; my vision had not changed. Now, easy as it might have been to slip back into that pit, I dug up all the courage and hope that I had not felt in a long time. I had my family around me, their support and their strength. I had Dad and my gift again. It was time to accept what would happen to me, whether in months, years or longer. It was poetic almost, closing in on ironic, that I was losing my physical sight while my 'second sight' continued to flourish.

3

As if losing my sight and my whole world changing because of it wasn't enough for one 18-year-old to handle, I was also ready to tell Mum and the world that I was gay. A gay blind medium? You really couldn't make it up. When I told Mum, the moment passed without pain or anger or disappointment. There was nothing but love and acceptance.

Ready to get back to some semblance of typical 18-year-old life, I began to socialise again, to go to parties and clubs, to see friends and meet new people. One night, at a local nightclub, a 21st birthday was in full swing. The birthday boy I half-knew and knew of his brother, and knew his brother's girlfriend. Bumping into people you kind of know, friends you've not seen in a while, in a club, we got to chatting, the small talk you have to shout over the ear-splitting bass of the music. Mark, the birthday boy, called us over. Instantly, I was struck by how handsome he was: his wonderful smile and his shy personality.

In communities like The Port, everyone knows everyone a little bit – it is always so-and-so's daughter, or your man McDonald, or the wee lassie over the road who married the altar boy who was in the crash with the boy whose maw was the art teacher. It turns out that our lives had been running parallel for a long time; living streets apart, same school bus, we'd been running in similar circles for years, only now overlapping. We got to chatting, then to flirting, and then to dating.

I have already said that I am not a fan of words like 'destiny' but I cannot deny the signs that appeared, hinting that Mark and I had been brought together. When Mark and Mum met for the first time, our world got smaller again.

'Is he a Morrison or an O'Neil?' Mum asked.

'A Morrison.'

'And who are his parents? Who are his grandparents?' All these questions Mum would fire at me while I had to quickly text Mark for the answers.

Living two streets away and going to a neighbouring school was not enough of a sign, it turned out that my great-grandfather was Mark's grandfather's boss. They had worked together and become friends - there is even a picture of Mark's mum holding Mum as a baby. Not only were Mark and I brought together, but two families, already with a long, loving history, were bound together.

Through it all, I kept my condition and my mediumship from Mark secret. With my mediumship, the last thing you want is to spill the spiritual beans. On every date, they're wondering whether someone is whispering in your ear. The alternative: they were too into it, asking every second whether some relative was watching them. And can you imagine trying to sleep with someone thinking a spirit was in the room? Yikes.

Talk about a passion killer. All I told Mark was that there were certain nights when I would be unavailable.

I was still dealing with my condition too, learning to navigate my life with my failing sight. While you are on cloud nine, dating someone new, someone you really like, the last thing you want is baggage to weigh you down. And that's how I saw my condition. No, I thought, I won't say anything just yet. My sight was failing, not totally gone. I could get away with it for a little bit longer.

Unfortunately, divine timing intervened, insisting that I no longer keep it a secret. Because of the genetic and hereditary nature of my condition, the doctors wanted to know who else might be affected. But with little to no information about my grandmother's adoption, we were at a loss. Eventually, Mum decided to reach out to the local newspaper, The Greenock Telegraph. They ran a story on me and my condition, hoping that something might click for someone, somewhere. The only person that it 'clicked' with was Mark. A guest at the hotel Mark worked at had left a copy of the newspaper. Picking it up, Mark read the headline splashed across the front page.

'I didn't want to involve you in all my shit,' I said when he called. 'I thought you might run for the hills or something.'

But Mark refused to budge. Even as I revealed the hurting parts of myself to him, as I overcame my pride and truly let him in, Mark and I became closer. So close that before I knew it, he had moved in with Mum and me.

Despite my vision, I was desperate to keep my independence and lead as ordinary a life as possible. Well, as ordinary as a visually impaired medium could be. And what do ordinary people do? They move out with their boyfriend. Mark and I moved into our first house, the biggest step I had taken in a long time. My sight posed just a few problems, hiccups in my everyday life. Mum wasn't there to clean up after me and to make sure I was wearing my clothes the right way round, and Mark was at work. I forced myself to acclimatise to my new surroundings, to trust in myself and in what sight I had to get by.

Moments would drift in occasionally, moments of darkness that I would have to fight through. Often, they were triggered by limitations of my sight – missing or not noticing things, like the floating, upturned very dead fish that I might have accidentally killed. Work tasks became harder, and I would become increasingly frustrated and miserable. The simple things that I used to be able to do were now mammoth tasks.

The darkness could be so thick and overwhelming at times. For a space of time, I thought what would happen if I stepped in front of the bus rather than on it? Yes, looking back I know it would have been selfish to act on any of those impulses. At the time though, there sometimes seemed no better way to cope. As they always had, Mum, Grandma, the rest of my family, and now Mark would reach out their hands and pull me out of my despair.

Living with a boyfriend alone for the first time, I was still reluctant to share my mediumship with Mark. Learning that your partner has a possibly permanent disability, however understanding you are, is one thing. Learning that said partner can also speak to the dead is on a whole other playing field. I was falling in love with Mark, now living with him. I was trying to maintain this persona, the outgoing glitzy Dom. To share my gift with Mark, I feared, would be too much. If I was in Mark's shoes and my partner told me they could speak to the dead, I would think they were barking mad. How do you tell someone, let them experience your gift, without looking or sounding like a crazy person? Naturally, I did my best to ease him in.

After several months of living together, Mark began asking questions about where I disappeared off to on Tuesday and Thursday evenings. Where was I going, what was I doing, who was I with, and how long would I be? Time to 'fess up. I told him that I was attending a Spiritualist church and that it was helping me develop my mediumship because I could speak to the dead.

'Alright, if that's what you believe, I'll leave you to it. Just don't go bringing any ghosts home with you, however friendly!' he grinned. Sounds like someone had watched 'Ghost' a few too many times.

He asked some questions, mostly your standard medium FAQs - what is it about? How do you do it? Sometimes he would come home while I was conducting a reading. But, as promised, he mostly left me to it.

That was until one night, lying in bed with Mark, a spirit made his presence known. Whenever a spirit wishes to interact with me, I will receive a calling card, a little indicator of a present spirit. I hadn't meant to make a noise.

'What is it? What do you see? Is someone there?' Mark asked.

'I've just seen a young man. I think he belongs to you.' I reeled off all the details I could of the young man's spirit. He was tall with short hair and a pierced eyebrow, with an M name: Martin, Michael or something, maybe even Michael Martin together. I was able to tell Mark every single detail of this spirit, right down to how he passed.

A shocked gasp was Mark's first reaction. Knowing and kind of believing your partner's a medium is very different from experiencing it first-hand. Listening to them talk about your cousin who passed five years ago, who they'd never met, is untrodden territory. Most couples go through their trials, with life testing how solid the relationship is. Few couples are tested by how well one partner receives a medium reading from the other. This could've been a minefield, my stepping too close to emotional wounds.

But I tried to pass it off as something happy, a close relative who in death was still with and looking out for him. For Mark, it was an intense and very real eye-opener. There was no questioning or doubt or healthy scepticism anymore. The details I'd given Mark were too specific, too personal, to disbelieve. Closer now to a 'true believer' Mark sometimes came to the Spiritualist church with me, watching me teach and truly being in my element. I was finally able to share the whole of my life with Mark.

Now that I wasn't keeping my gift a secret from him, I was no longer so cautious about sharing it with other people. Yes, there were people in my life who knew about my gift, and their eyes would roll with pound signs, but only for themselves. Management companies took advantage. Friends expected free readings, calling me every hour of the day and night to talk about another dead relative or ask for tomorrow night's winning lottery numbers. But more often than not, sharing my gift was healing and treated with respect.

More eyes and minds were opened to my mediumship once we moved in with Mark's mum, Liz. Our own house was only temporary, and Liz welcomed us into her home, and me into her family. She quickly became somewhat of a second mother to me.

'I've had readings and visited psychics before, but I just don't know,' Liz said as we sat around the breakfast bar at Mum's.

'Shame you broke the toaster this morning,' I said.

'But how could you know?'

'And that cruise? What's stopping you from booking it?'

Nothing scary or awful or too personal came from the psychic reading I gave Liz that night, and she began to open up. It was still early days for Mark and me, and I didn't want to chance my luck with a full spiritual reading. But that little push, that taste of what I could do, was enough to clear away any scepticism for Liz. So much so that she began helping out at the Voice of Spirit Centre when I opened it. She lent a hand where she could, serving tea and cake, but hiding at the back during readings, still a little afraid of a full reading.

Mark learnt about my failing vision, and then he learnt about my gift. It was not simply knowing about them, but he was living and experiencing them, the joys and the obstacles, through me. And he still stayed with me. Eleven years later, he might call himself a dogsbody, chauffeur, manager and the rest, but I do not know what I would do or where I would be without him. Our relationship continued to blossom. As did my gift, going from strength to strength, learning more and more skills at the centre. I was truly becoming tuned in to Spirit.

4

As my sight continued to decline and my gift for mediumship continued, I found myself at a crossroads. Behind me were the pain and depression of my condition, and finding my feet as a medium. Before me, who knew? And like the bundled pack of The Fool tarot card, I was carrying my passion, my pain and knowledge forward, stepping into an unknown future. What would my next steps be?

By late December 2010, my employer was still adapting the office to help me; every support and scheme was implemented, from adapted screens to taking a taxi to work rather than the bus. As thankful as I was, answering the phones to customers every day, slipping my psychic impressions in as small talk, I knew this was not my passion. Or in the parlance of spiritualism, this was not my destiny, not what I was 'called' to do. I was attending church, climbing the platform whenever I could, using my gift to help and heal; but something this special, this potentially powerful, I couldn't continue to relegate to a simple pastime. The time had arrived for me to embrace my mediumship full-time.

You could not find a more non-traditional or unconventional career path. I would not be clocking in every day at 9 am; would not be engaging in any water cooler chit-chat; there'd be no chipping in for a colleague's birthday present and the customers would be of a very different calibre. I would be describing a memory, whispered in my ear, to prove that I was talking to Spirit, not trying to explain a bill. Daunting as it might have been, I had the full belief and support of my family and my friends and the network of the spiritualist community; customers who trusted and valued my ability, and fellow mediums who recommended me.

A typical day would start at around 1 pm. I am not, never have been and never will be a morning person. Everyone knows I will not take any clients until at least after lunch. Spirits might not sleep, but I certainly need mine. I would take my time to prepare for each reading and the evening demonstration. Mark's mum would come in, help with the teas and coffees and sandwiches. (Who knew healing and being healed by Spirit could be such thirsty work?)

While it was vastly different from any ordinary job, losing that structure of being here and there at a specific time, I developed a good rhythm to my days. The more I worked, the more I was recommended, and the more my days would fill up with readings and classes. There was rarely a quiet day, even early on.

While the church provided me with all the training and practice that I needed to use my gift, I wanted to strike out on my own and form my own Spiritualist church. It became a passion project. All the confidence I had lost from my condition, all the confidence I had gained from my gift and time at the church, culminated in creating this space. I wanted to open doors for people as the doors of the Butterfly Centre had been opened for me. I had never set foot in a Spiritualist church before and, not to over-exaggerate, it changed me. If I could open a door for someone, someone hurting or broken, someone grieving or mourning, and offer them a healing hand, then the project would've been worthwhile. I wanted to be the roof over someone's head, the hand they held, and the voice that healed them. If the church was the tree that I had grown on, then my own church was the seed it had produced, and I was ready to tend it.

Hours were spent researching, trawling every corner of the internet to find a suitable building. One of my main stipulations was that I wanted it to be based in Greenock. Though I am not from Greenock, I have always considered it my spiritual home – maybe the only person who has considered it so – and knew I wanted to set up shop there. Plus, there was no Spiritualist church or centre there, so I wouldn't be stepping on anyone's toes. See, already business savvy!

Our first premise was an old dance hall. With Mark and Liz helping out, we set up shop. By December, The Voice of Spirit Spiritualist church was open. Growing my mediumship from a gift and hobby, however profound, to a full-time job meant learning the business ropes alongside giving readings. Nothing helps sell a business like a catchy name. No deliberation or discussion was necessary when it came to the name, The Voice of Spirit. It was Dad's voice that had begun my journey, and the voice of Spirit that guided me. The name, the church and my gift, all were done in the service of sharing that voice. It would be shared when I performed on the platform, when I conducted private readings and, as I planned, when I helped others nurture their own mediumship abilities. I had such big plans.

But the building was too big and too cold. Even all the warmth of Spirit's messages couldn't heat the place. That, as well as some aggressive neighbours, told me that it was time to move on and find a new and better space. I still wanted to share the voice of Spirit, to open the door to all people, those interested in mediumship and those who needed the comfort of Spirit's messages. I just needed to find a new door.

We found a new spot for the centre, a church hall in Greenock where I had always wanted to base it. We were better suited here, and when we opened, attendance continued to grow. Here, I was able to explore my passion to teach and start the development group I wanted, teaching and encouraging other local mediums. This began to grow too; mediums and prospective psychics would arrive from further afield, looking to hone their skills. Establishing my own Spiritualist church cemented my place within the community too. As the church became more popular, and as I and the way I worked became more popular, I began to get bookings from other churches around the country. Word of mouth had led them to The Voice of Spirit.

Another move to above Smith's meant we could establish not only a workplace for me but a kind of 'spiritualist hub' in Greenock. We attracted mediums, therapists and healers of every variety. We could sell crystals and jewellery, and we even hosted the odd craft fair. But an unpleasant neighbour with whom we shared a communal door spelt a final move to Jamacia Street.

You could only have described the place as a bombsite. Starting from the ground up, we tore the place apart to remake it in my desired image. And the centre continued to be successful; loyal attendees seemed happy to follow me to every weird and wonderful location, as did class attendees. More established mediums would visit, teaming up with me to demonstrate and teach. And every new site, every new location, we were on someone else's doorstep, just waiting for the right fateful wind to blow them inside.

Still, I felt limited here. We would open Sundays and Mondays, and every Thursday was dedicated to the development group. There were always more people to reach. Without sounding too much like a missionary, I wanted to help and offer my gift to as many people as I could. Every day, I was witness to the blessings and comfort that messages from Spirit could provide. But people had to choose to come to me; some spurred on by friends or family, some who had always had a fascination with spiritualism, and some who were grieving and would try anything to hear from a loved one. Occasionally, and always the stories I love to hear the most, people would tell me how they had been led to me, under strange almost destined circumstances, like something from a movie. Leaflets blowing in the wind, pop-up adverts on social media that they'd never seen before, or chance encounters with old friends on their way to see me.

The development of each venue had eaten away at my earnings and my savings. With the increased demand both at the centre and for touring, Mark had to quit his job to manage me full-time. More and more, and for longer and longer I was away from the centre. And while I had built up a trusty staff, it wasn't fair to be leaving them to it, to have them work on the dream project that I had created. Eight years since I had opened The Voice of Spirit, I had helped and healed, and I felt that I had done my part, especially for Greenock. We closed the centre in 2018.

In my mind, I'd always had this little fantasy of having a wee New Age shop, with shelves of crystals and tarot cards, and always the faint whiff of incense. So, when there was the opportunity to have such a stall in the Savoy Centre in Glasgow, I couldn't sign the lease fast enough. You could barely swing a cat in the lot we were given, room enough for a table, chairs and a curtained-off section for private readings. Mum and Mark helped set it up, decorate and find stock from wholesalers. And the place was ready.

A wee stall of my own; people would no longer have to make the dedicated trip to the church. I could read for every Average Joe in town, taking a breather between shopping or going for drinks or having dinner.

Knowing the Savoy Centre, its notoriety and reputation, I prepared myself to meet every possible type of wacky, weird and wonderful person.

From the church, I had gained confidence in my gifts, confidence that people *wanted* me to read for them. Yet, in this new environment, there was some doubt that gnawed at the back of my mind. Opening the stall at 23, I was worried my age might undermine the whole endeavour. Who had ever heard of a 23-year-old medium? Who wanted a 23-year-old medium to read for them? I was younger than the average age of the common Savoy Centre visitor and probably younger than what most of them would expect a medium to be. After all the experience I'd gained, the money I'd saved for the lease and the preparations I'd made, I began to worry whether anyone would come at all.

But it was clear this was where I was supposed to be. The day I signed the lease, I was sitting in a café inside the Centre with Liz and having a spot of lunch, when a gentleman spirit made himself known. Usually, I can 'switch it off', placing boundaries between the times I allow and don't allow spirits to approach. Sometimes I have to be stern with spirits, instructing them to back off when I am not working, unless it is life and death; sometimes, I have to call on Dad to escort spirits into 'the wings'. If their message is that important, they'll be patient. As it turned out, this was life or death.

The gentleman continued to try and grab my attention, refusing to back off. Eventually, Dad's voice whispered in my ear, instructing me to help this man. There was no getting out of this now.

'I need you to give my wife a message,' the gentleman said.

'You'll need to give me some details if I'm going to convince a complete stranger,' I said. He reeled off as many details as he could, solid proof that would hopefully convince his wife that the totally random guy disturbing her day was speaking to her dead husband.

'Okay, so who is your wife?'

'The woman with the umbrella,' the gentleman replied. It was summer and the weather had been nothing but sunny all day. Was this spirit pulling my leg or just confused? Just as I was about to ask the gentleman to clarify, through the doors burst a woman, accompanied by a man and woman, fighting with an umbrella. They were laden with bags, clearly post-shopping spree, looking for food and shelter from the sudden unseasonable downpour. That time had come to spring into action.

With the gentleman spirit close, I approached the woman, apologising for interrupting her day.

'This will sound really weird but I'm a medium, and your husband has approached me because he needs to pass on a message.' I repeated all the information the gentleman had given me, trying to prove myself and my gift before this poor woman called security over.

'He wants me to tell you that you must continue, that you must keep going for your kids and that he is there with you.' As soon as I had finished speaking, she began to cry. Naturally, many cry when receiving a message from Spirit, but I felt especially bad having hijacked this woman's family day out and made her grieve in the middle of the Savoy Centre.

I returned to my table, but the woman followed. 'I have to thank you,' she said, turning to look at her children. She then explained that she had taken her children out for the day, spoiling them, doing anything she could to create a lasting happy memory for them. Because, she went on, she had decided that after the day out, she would go home and take her own life so that she could join her husband.

'I am just struggling without him, and I'm finding it so hard to cope. But you, you have given me the strength not to go through with it.'

It was an absolute goosebumps moment. You would think with the gifts I have, after reading for people from every walk of life, with more stories than could fill a library, the personal impact, the gobsmacked awe I feel when people respond like this, would diminish over time. But when events unfold like this, when the effects a person feels from a reading are so immediate and essential, it bowls me over. The tiny hidden mechanics of the universe; the lot being available, my wanting to take it and saving the money, my being there that day to sign the lease, had been toiling away to ensure this happened. The divine timing, like a giant cosmic clock, had been just right. Nothing could persuade me now that this wasn't where I was supposed to be. Nothing could persuade me I didn't have work to do here.

As expected, some readings, some people, were less positive, even downright unsavoury. I try not to make too many assumptions, but when you can read a person from a mile off, the creeping feeling up your spine, you worry where the reading might go. Once, I had two gentlemen come for a reading. Typical Glaswegian 'hard men' with tattooed necks and thick gold chains who looked like they could break bricks with their bare hands; far and away from my typical customers. There was no way I could refuse to read for these men and I tried not to judge them. Maybe they would have the charity of the Six of Pentacles, or a spirit would come through looking to thank these men.

Cautiously, I invited the first gentleman back for his reading. Shuffling and laying out my tarot cards, listening and reading, I described a court case that the gentleman was involved in. Here we go, I thought. When reading tarot cards as opposed to a medium reading, I get a little more time before I have to speak – a minute, seconds really, where I can convince the customer that I'm checking over my insights. My reading style is as much about each card's meaning as it is about intuition, connecting with the person. If the cards are a code, then connecting with each querent cracks the code. In that precious time, I can begin to think about how I am going to approach the reading.

Justice, The Two of Cups, The Fool; this gentleman was involved in a court case, and was literally being taken for a fool. Between a witness's testimony and being thrown under the bus by another party, the case was not going in the gentleman's favour. Drugs and lots of money were involved. I advised him to keep his friends close, but his enemies closer.

The next gentleman followed. Again, I shuffled, laid out and read the cards. Well, what do you know- it looked like he was the one ready to throw his companion, or rather accomplice, under the bus. Proof positive that you never know who is going to come for a reading.

It's rare that I have readings like I did for the two gentlemen, readings that oppose one another or are so interconnected. However, readings with unexpected or 'piggyback' spirits happen more often. A customer will come for a reading, but a spirit might sneak through, only partially linked to the customer, hoping that a message can be passed on.

Ultimately, I had to end my time at the stall. I was travelling and touring more, and I didn't have the time or energy the stall deserved. But whenever I do go to Glasgow, and pass the Centre, I think and remember the shop I had. I remember the people I met, and the readings I gave, and always thank it, thank Spirit, for the many doors it opened for me.

My stall at the Savoy Centre was not the only door that swung open for me, bringing me a vast array of opportunities. Being a young, visually impaired medium who had begun his own Spiritualist church, was newsworthy. A journalist from The Scottish Sun, named Yvonne Bolouri, reached out to Mark, looking to have a reading and write a piece on me. Ever the one to blether with, well, anyone, I was more than happy to oblige.

Both the reading and the interview went great, and the article was wonderful. It was very much a stick-it-on-the-fridge moment of pride. What I had not expected was Yvonne to reach out again. The article had done so well, she said, that she wanted to offer me a weekly column. My first response was that I would love to. *No way*, was my second more practical thought. How could I do that, write anything, with my sight making it a struggle? I had never really written anything before, and being a good talker does not always translate into being a good writer. Besides the practical concerns, there were psychic ones to consider too. I had never read or done anything psychic this way, through letters or emails. I had always relied on my sight, on talking to people and having my messages confirmed. How could I do that in a column?

I voiced my doubts to Yvonne, nervous about whether something like this would really work. She was nothing but accommodating. That's what editors are for, she explained. There would be plenty of people to help me out. I was given a two-week trial period, to see how it worked for me and whether it worked for Yvonne.

With Mark's help, I began to pick emails and letters and respond to them. How I was to 'read' via letters and emails still played on my mind. Would I be able to tap into each sender's situation and link with Spirit to receive a message? With face-to-face readings, I can connect with the querent, read their energy and listen to whatever spirit comes forward. I can get real-time validation which is a confidence boost. Instead, I had to trust myself, my gift and Spirit; I was throwing caution to the wind.

As I should have known, all I had to do was ask Spirit, ask how I could deliver these messages. Whenever I received a letter, I would ask Spirit aloud what this person needed to know, whether there was a spirit with a message. Sometimes I would pull a tarot card or two. I would reach out to Spirit, trying to feel the emotion in the letter, and Spirit always reached back. Even with the vast array of situations I was asked about – from lost cats to difficult divorces – I was still able to relay insightful and evidential messages, as the responses were fantastically positive.

Having passed the trial period short of any hiccups, I wrote for The Sun for five years. Sometimes it would be in the classic Agony Aunt style, answering questions that readers sent in. But with the success of the column, I was given free rein, able to explore all manner of psychic topics, through my gift and my writing. I pulled tarot cards for celebrities; I visited infamously haunted Scottish sites, investigating whether a medium's approach might shed some light on the stories; I would talk about the day-to-day life of being a medium and all that it entailed. For five years, I had a dedicated page in the Sunday issue. How many 21-year-olds can say that they've discovered their mediumship abilities, begun running their own Spiritualist church, and had their own column in a national newspaper?

The appetite for Spiritualism continued to grow, and a weekly column could only do so much. So of course, it didn't stop at just the weekly column. Social media accounts were set up, and I was doing livestream readings, replying to messages. No two days were the same, just as no two questions, answers or spirits were. I felt like an advice columnist, someone you would see in a film, lending a hand to total strangers. Only I had a bit of an edge – I had Spirit as my co-worker. The advice I gave was relayed from Spirit, maybe a friend or relative who had passed, problems only they could have specific insight on. I didn't know whether this reader should leave their job or that reader should be stricter with their children. But a grandmother might, remind the reader of their childhood dream and how resilient they are. A close friend might recall all the times and ways the reader was an amazing parent. All I could do was relay those messages.

For three years, 52 editions each year, I went through each email, picked out what I could, and cleared the overspilling inbox of the rest. For three years, I researched haunted places in Scotland – not gimmicky ones, but ones that could be proved, impressions that could be validated. For three years, I scanned the news for relevant celebrities, picking tarot cards to see what was in the stars for, well, the stars. For three years, I like to think I was of service in a different way. Not everyone could make the journey to a reading or the centre, but most could pen a letter or an email. Would I do it again? Probably not. Was it an unforgettable insightful experience? Absolutely.

While my time at the Savoy Centre had brought people to me, my column had brought me to the people. However, my feet were beginning to itch. My column could only reach so far. Those who did come to my shows or write to the column were those who perhaps knew about me and what I do or had some belief in mediumship. To heal and help as many as I could, even the sceptics, I would need to travel further afield. If they couldn't come to me, I would have to go to them.

5

Through my column, I began to receive invitations to visit this town and that city. I might be able to reach one person with a private reading or in a column for a Sunday paper, but a whole show, several shows? The potential to heal, to give as many messages from Spirit as possible, would be huge. The want for shows was there, and I was just as keen. Signing off my column, endlessly grateful for the possibilities it bestowed on me and the way it honed my gifts, I was ready to reply to these invitations. And the 'Voice of Spirit' tour was born.

My first mini-tour as it were, came very unexpectedly. Sure, there was a voice in the back of my head, a wish I had, that I could start doing events further from home, but I hadn't the infrastructure just yet.

While I was still at the Savoy, a group of girls travelled to Glasgow for a shopping trip. Somehow, they ended up at the Savoy; somehow, they ended up coming to my stall for a reading. One girl came straight in, clearly eager for a reading. But, under Spirit's guidance, the reading wasn't really for her. A spirit approached me, giving me all the information that I needed. When I began to relay the message, she was shocked. She instantly recognised the spirit as her friend's brother who had taken his own life. Their connection was that she had reported it and helped her friend as much as anyone could during that time.

In a way that only Spirit could devise, that reading opened a door for me. Years later, I received a message on Facebook from someone I neither knew nor recognised.

'Did you once have a shop in the Savoy Centre?' she wrote.

I replied that yes, some years ago I did. As it turns out, it was the girl I had read for on that trip. Ever since then, she explained, she had been attempting to find me, searching for me on the internet, Googling me under the name of Damian, although where she got that name from I don't know. We chatted for a while. When she had returned to Campbeltown, she had talked about the reading to anyone who would listen, and sung my praises to all and sundry.

Now that she had found me, she begged for me to come and visit. Under ordinary circumstances, travelling to a different town invited by someone you had met once, who had subsequently been trying to find you on the Internet for several years, would be ill-advised. But this was Spirit's divine timing. This girl was supposed to find me again, and I knew I should accept her invitation. Details swapped, plans made, and suddenly I was performing in Campbeltown.

Leanne, the visitor at the Savoy, arranged the entire thing, from booking halls, organising readings, and setting me up in a hotel. In all honestly, I had never heard of Campbeltown, and could not point to it on a map. But when I discovered it was a small rural town, this filled me with some anxiety. Would there be enough people to fill a hall? Would there be any private readings booked? Would all the readings be about selling cows and catching fish? It could have gone either way.

The shows that we organised sold out. The readings were fully booked and the live streams were inundated with comments and questions and people asking about loved ones or waiting for a name they recognised. Even after confirming that all the readings' spaces were filled, Leanne continued to receive requests. All my anxieties were put to bed.

I experienced and gave some intense one-of-a-kind readings during that first trip to Campbeltown. One reading I gave to a woman described her father who had been in a head-on collision. But there had been a younger person with him too. Sure enough, her father and brother had been in a car accident on their way to work.

'And I keep seeing a helicopter, like round and round and round. Does that mean anything?'

I had never seen something like this before, and I could not make sense of it. As it turned out, the father and brother were airlifted to a Glasgow hospital. To make this small world even smaller, I told the woman that I kept seeing a certain row of houses in Greenock. Greenock was where her family had come from originally.

With many readings, more and more bizarre, phenomenal and specific connections were being made. I could be giving one person a reading, passing a message on from their sister, for example, then a shout or a raised hand would shoot up from the back; this person's brother had been engaged to the first person's sister. More than usual, I had to watch what I said. In these small villages, everyone knew someone who knew someone. Every other year, I still return to Campbeltown, feeling like I can masquerade as a local celebrity. The locals know me and I know them. And every time, the audiences and the halls get bigger.

This was what I had wanted to do, to travel and keep reaching people, further and further away. I had gone from the regular congregations of the Spiritualist church, invited to churches and centres elsewhere, to have a stall in the Savoy Centre, where anyone could walk in for a reading. And now, touring towns and cities.

Despite the successes of my shows in Campbeltown, there remained persisting anxiety and apprehension. I was so used to one-on-one readings with no interference, spiritual or otherwise, where I could delve deep into the details. At the Spiritualist churches, the audiences were not so large as to be overwhelming, but on a tour, selling out whole halls and hotel rooms? The pressure to prove myself, to supply evidentiary messages, mounted with every ticket bought. Sure, the demand for messages, for healing, was clearly there, but what of the supply? Would I be able to read for such a large audience?

Before every tour, before every show, I have to remind myself of my faith in Spirit; remind myself and then practise it. Spirit had never, would never, abandon me; Spirit had come through every time. Performance anxiety was the root of it all, nothing else. My messages are proof, not only for the clients but for me. I reassured myself, I can do this.

By travelling around the country, I was meeting – some might say released on – more people, not solely in quantity but also in quality. Attendees came from all backgrounds and walks of life. Some had been long-time believers in mediumship and spiritualism, whilst others were sceptical, staunch naysayers who had been dragged along in hopes of a point being proved wrong. While it has never been my aim to say 'I told you so', if they were able to gain something from a visit, even if that was simply by stepping a little bit closer to believing, I could not ask for more.

And in turn, people attending found themselves exposed to a world they had so far been apart from. They might have been to a church, and read their horoscope once, but watching a medium? Not only do my shows open up a world to people, I like to think I'm offering something different from what they might have known or believed before.

Mediumship offers an alternative view on death, life-after-death and spirits from other paths and faiths. When I teach or perform, I might say that a spirit has passed on, but I try to emphasise that they are still alive in Spirit, that they have a life that continues, and that those spirits watch us, listen to us, and can communicate with us. There is nothing dogmatic or judgemental about what I do and how I portray my mediumship. There is no one burning in Hell. The most they might do is cause a little mischief and push me to say something embarrassing.

In every tour, I include a show in Greenock, my spiritual home, sometimes starting there as I did for my first tour. From there, I try to hit various towns and cities, somewhere central that people don't mind travelling a little while to. Every destination has its own people and culture and nuances that I enjoy watching, especially in the context of readings. People in Edinburgh don't react like people in Inverness, who don't react like people in Aberdeen or Falkirk.

Once I get over my fears and worries about performances, which I still get several years on, I allow Spirit to enter, listen to them and speak for them. While a bigger audience can mean more worry for me, it also provides a big pond to fish out bigger stories. The further I go, the more people watching me, the wackier and wilder the connections, and the more profound and powerful the messages and healing can be.

In Falkirk once, a father spirit showed me a whole set of Snow White garden ornaments. It was confirmed that these same ornaments, down to each dwarf, were now at his grave. In Inverness, another father spirit kept showing me an image of Elvis (dad jokes and typical paternal mischief, I can confirm, continue in Spirit). Naturally, this was giggle-worthy and I could not make head nor tail of it. But between laughs, the mother and daughter were able to say that he had been an Elvis tribute act. At least he didn't make me try to sing! While messages like these can be funny and I always encourage some laughter at my shows, they still mean something to someone.

With audiences of 80, 90, 100 and more, there is still only one of me. I wish that I could give every single person - those in mourning, those who need healing - a message that their loved ones are with them, especially those who've travelled far. It would be impossible to do that; I would be there for days.

For people who don't receive a connection, I have seen the profound effect of simply being present when someone else receives a message. It can become undeniable, watching an audience member nod their head to details, and cry, laugh or both to memories that I share through Spirit. True, it might not create die-hard converts, but maybe it is a little step towards belief, baby steps towards healing of their own. If one audience member's loved one can come through, then surely anyone else's can too. It just might not be their time.

Every show on every tour that I do, I am putting down roots. Not only am I leaving audiences with messages, but also with my name. That first tour was so important for me, to spread my wings across the country. Yes, in my little corner of Scotland, I had made a name for myself. Through my gift, I built a reputation that had people following me from centre to centre, with clients returning over and over.

Performing in these new towns and cities, I was able to plant the seeds of what I can do, watering it with performances and private readings. Through that, my reputation has become established. I have become a perennial visitor to particular spots, where the communities have embraced me. Now, not only do I have returning clients in Greenock, but all over the place. One year, it would be a person on their own; the next year, they'd come with pals; they'd bring their grannies the next year, who'd bring their pals the following year. On and on it goes. I must be doing something right.

With years of touring the same places, I know all the little intimate connections, who's married to whose cousin, who used to work with whose father, who was in a car accident. Names become familiar, and I know all the best spots for coffee or a glass of wine. Romanticising what I do is simple, declaring it a calling, a destiny or such, but at the end of the day, it is still a business.

Touring comes with many varied benefits for me, as both a business and a working medium. Sure, it is nice to travel and have returning clients, the ebb and flow of performance anxiety and reassurance in my gift, especially through feedback. But it has helped me grow and evolve as a medium too.

Away from my comfort zone spots and typical methods, I can test new techniques, changing how I approach and relay messages. When I first began to lose my sight and develop my clairaudience, it was during my tours that I gained confidence. Each time I worked this way, especially in an unfamiliar setting, asking for and waiting for a spirited whisper in my ear, Spirit was telling me, 'Yes, you can work this way.' Practice makes perfect, but it also built my confidence with this newer methodology.

One particular reading in Grangemouth during a tour helped reassure me that clairaudience would work and that my gift was not lost with my sight. In one of the shows, a woman and her two pals had won a VIP session, including front-row seats and a 20-minute private reading. During the show, a woman came through for them, a friend or sister, perhaps 53 or 54-ish with a Sh- name, and some connection to Benidorm. As with most messages, there was a mixture of gasps, tears and laughter. The woman had lost her sister Shannon just before a planned trip to Benidorm. She and her pals had still gone, and, I was told, they had written her name in the sand and taken a picture.

'How could you know that?' they asked.

I don't know it, or see it as some mediums do, I simply listen.

As much as I love returning to Greenock and towns close by, conducting private readings and teaching, touring is such a passion. Truly, it has become one of the building blocks of my mediumship. Touring for the first time, attempting to read new people in new places with perhaps very little knowledge of mediumship was daunting. Now, it is second nature.

Every year, I look forward to touring getting underway: planning the route, the hotels and booking the private readings. And, not to toot my own horn, but the people keep coming. The need and desire for healing, for messages from loved ones, is infinite. Let's just say, I am not worried about going out of business any time soon. And that demand is worldwide. I know my way around this country, am known on the circuit and have a steady flow of clients. Like many British-born personalities, no matter the field, the logical next step was to break America.

Arlene's Story

Since I was a girl, I had been aware of Spirit. As I grew up, I began to dip my toe into Spiritualism. I attended various churches and centres, listened to people talking and talking to Spirit, and read everything I could get my hands on. One evening, my pal Kirsty and I went to the Lighthouse Spiritualist Church in Greenock. Kirsty pointed out Dominic to me. According to her, he was beginning to make a name for himself as a medium. I was intrigued.

After the demonstration, I went up to Dom and asked about development classes; where and when and if I could attend. I hoped that Dom saw me as a suitable candidate. With no Sorting Hat like in *Harry Potter*, I prayed he could see something in me, that I would be chosen. I was fascinated by this world of spirits. I had known death and was not necessarily frightened of it. He welcomed me with open arms and an open mind.

On the first night that I attended the circle, there were about 10 or 12 other students. To begin with, Dom took us through a series of preliminary exercises, I guess to ready us. Then came the first exercise. Dom placed a piece of paper on the floor and told us all to imagine this was the stage we would demonstrate on. As soon as our feet touched that stage, we would connect with Spirit. This is the deep end, I thought, and I'll admit, I was nervous. This was a whole new level of spiritualism to me. I was no longer a spectator but a participant, and I began to wonder what I had gotten myself into. There were doubts too, not as to whether this was real, but whether I could do it.

When it was my turn to step onto the paper platform, I was a bag of nerves. Dom told me to take a deep breath, that I should relax and ask my loved ones to come forward. After all, it was only my first class. Readying myself, I stepped forward onto the paper. Instantly, I was pulled by something and took a step back, almost off the paper. Dom explained that a pull forward indicates a female spirit, backwards a male. I repositioned myself on the paper and continued. Dom asked me what I felt and if I could begin to hear or see anything. I told the class that I could feel something in my solar plexus, like when a car goes over a speed bump. Then, a nervous sensation, one I didn't recognise as my own. I was connected to the spirit world.

Feeling stronger and more prepared, I journeyed further and further into the connection. I was on a tarmacked path, not quite a road, and bordered by grass on both sides. I was panicking and running for my life. I looked around the room, searching for help. Then I was breathing heavily, my legs turned to jelly, and I felt a sharp pain in my heart. There was no question what had happened; there was no sensing or guessing, no hunches or maybes, I knew that the spirit had been stabbed to death.

Such an experience was overwhelming and I never expected it, especially on my first go. Given my own history, it felt serendipitous that it was this spirit and the death of a young man that I experienced. Dom told me that Spirit had explained that I needed this particular experience, something perhaps close to the bone, to fully understand that Spirit was alive and very much around me.

I stepped off the paper, reeling from the mental, emotional and physical sensations of my connection. When I was ready, I was able to describe more of what I had seen and experienced during the connection. A young man, roughly in his 20s and dressed in dark clothing; he was of medium build and had dark hair. While no doubt this was accurate, Dom pushed me to see if I could describe any distinguishing features. Was there anything that stood out? I immediately remembered his eyebrows, they had several shaved lines in them.

I told the spirit to step back, to allow myself to return to my body and mind, just as Dom taught. Quickly, the sensation in my solar plexus was gone. Only later in the class did another student approach me and say that she knew the spirit, that I had described, he was her friend who had been stabbed to death.

In Dom's words, I had a natural knack for this and took to mediumship like a bird to flight. I definitely belonged here. That first connection was phenomenal; there was no chance I could forget it. I had found a path I was happy walking down and I was 100% ready to commit to the work. After that first class and experience, I began to trust Dom's process, happily throwing caution to the wind and believing in Spirit.

With each circle, I became stronger, and surer in myself and these abilities. Dom and others would come up to me, saying that this or that they'd felt too or recognised.

Despite this aptitude for mediumship I'd acquired, my 'real' life, in the end, had to come first. Was I going to change the world with what I could do? Shake things up for whole audiences and communities via mediumship? Maybe not, but Spirit was able to see the whole journey and steer me on this path. I learnt what I needed to learn, and gained the tools I needed, for myself and the people in my life. Through the confluence of my mediumship skills, my personal interactions and understanding of Spirit, and my compassion, I managed to apply my skills to my present life, though perhaps in a less glamourous way than Dom. Currently, I volunteer to help those in end-of-life care, being there for people who don't have families or friends. Dom's teaching, patience and kindness have given me gifts and insights that I never could've imagined. I carry them and him with me today.

Myself as a toddler aged 2,
most probably getting into some sort of mischief.

My Father, My hero captain of Greenock Morton FC
John Boag, who this book is dedicated to
and the true voice of spirit.

Back to where it all began for Mark & I in 2009.

Mark and I on a cruise in winter 2019
with our mothers, Rita & Elizabeth.

My sister Danielle and brother Stuart surprising me at my last home demonstration before my trip to America in August 2022.

My beautiful grandparents Alec & Margaret.
This photo was taken in their favourite place, Benidorm,
when myself & Mark took them away in April 2023.

Myself and Mary DiGiovanni in 2022.
This was the first time we had seen each other since 2019.
So much happened during that 3 years other than COVID,
and as you can see we are so happy to be back together.

Mark & I in America at our friend's wedding, September 2022.

6

After my first UK tour, overwhelmed with the response from audiences and the excitement, I felt I was ready to go again. Being on the road, finding people who needed healing, this was what I wanted to do, what I needed to do. I was almost like a doctor making house calls; not everyone can journey to me, so I have to travel to heal them. The opportunity that knocked on my door next took me across the ocean.

Through recommendations and contacts, I had the chance to travel to America, to read, perform at and visit Spiritual churches and centres. Truth be told, the prospect was quite intimidating. I didn't know how Spiritualism worked in America, the style of their readings or what their mediums were like. My gift had got me this far, and my faith in it remained unwavering, but that was only on this side of the Atlantic. I questioned how I would cope. Would they understand my accent? Would I understand them? Would my style of reading translate? The cultures and cliques of the American communities and States were unknown to me. What if I said or did the wrong thing?

Despite my fears, I could only accept the offer with open hands. On my trip out to the States, I had been booked and was hosted by Reverend Mary DiGiovanni, a pastor at the Greater Boston Church of Spiritualism. Booked on, let's face it, a bit of a whim. Mary had never seen me work and didn't know me very well; I had been recommended alongside another medium and she took a chance. And I am greatly indebted to her for that.

Arriving at the hotel, I was greeted by a lovely gift hamper from Mary, filled with all sorts of Boston memorabilia: Boston beans, a Boston t-shirt and a Boston Red Sox mug. A real taste of that famous American hospitality, I felt instantly welcomed and slightly more at ease. Or so I thought.

That first evening, there was a ticketed event at the church, around 60 people or so. As I waited in the wings with my suit, getting myself ready, I wondered what on earth I had signed myself up for. When it was my turn to take the stage, I introduced myself and explained a little about how I work. And of course, I had to explain that I was visually impaired. I did not know how that would go down. The bigger the audience, sometimes the less responsive. You will get the monosyllabic 'yes' and 'no' (or in Scotland an 'aye'), and people will nod their heads. I had to reiterate that putting hands up and waving would be no good, and they would need to shout out. All I could do- we could do, was to see how this went.

So, I began and got my first connection. I connected with a young girl in Spirit who had been in a vehicle accident, and I had the impression that the accident had happened in front of a fire house. Two friends recognised the girl. Instantly, I became aware of the changes in my language. It was 'vehicle' not 'car', 'fire house' instead of 'fire station'. Even my gift was attuning to the States.

The two friends said that they understood the details, that their friend Michelle had died in front of a fire house. I gave them more and more details, down to the street name where the accident happened. My first message in America, in a church in Boston, was great. They were blown away – if I say so myself.

So too was Mary, who said how impressed she was with my performance, especially being so young. In her mind, there was something special about me and how I worked; something of an old soul, she would say. Maybe because of my youth, she saw in me a bright sense of adventure, that I took great joy in being able to serve. She was right.

Mary herself describes Spirit and me as true working partners; one does not serve or command the other, we work in tandem. I trust in my gifts from Spirit and the divine timetable it works on. Spirit trusts that I will be in the right place at the right time, to pass on messages and make connections the best way I can. Being invited to America wasn't just an opportunity for me, but also for so many people who needed messages and healing. And without sounding too self-important or too mumbo-jumbo-ey, I trust that they needed these messages from me. Spirit made sure of that.

I remember reading for a young girl in Boston. Though you would never have guessed it by looking at her, my instant impression was this feeling of being weighed down, that her pain was a constant burden. Her brother came through for her.

'He's showing me a van, but the van isn't how he passed, or has nothing to do with his passing. The van is a concern, for you and the family, and it just keeps going on. Do you understand that?'

Sure enough, she did. Her brother had sold the van; I was able to tell her how much for. More and more information I gave, including everything her brother had seen and wanted to do since his passing, such as wanting to shake her partner's hand. After the reading, the young girl came up to me.

'I didn't know what to expect from this, from coming here,' she said. 'But I wanted to thank you. I'm leaving with my brother.' From Scotland, I had travelled and been led a long way to give her some closure over her loss.

Am I the only medium who could have delivered this message? No, I wouldn't say that. But do I believe that all the moving parts that had to slot into place, my visiting America, the young girl coming to the church that night, and her brother coming through, meant something? How could I not? I might have flown to the US by plane, but it was Spirit that brought me there.

In private readings too, I felt this strong sense of purpose, that some sort of divine intervention, some hand had drawn my path and that of others together. We collided and met under ideal circumstances. And sometimes people can be driving along that path for a while. Once, a woman drove two hours to attend a private reading with me, a person, she knew nothing about.

During the reading, her mother's spirit came through to comfort and reassure her daughter, a message I was more than willing to relay. Overwhelmed with guilt and pain, the woman had been splitting her time between New York and Boston, between caring for her sick mother and being with her husband and son. She was exhausted.

'I'm okay, don't worry about me,' the mother wanted me to say. 'Get yourself back on track.' It was the message that the woman needed for her to heal and for closure. She now could focus on and look after herself. After the reading, she left hurriedly. Days later, she returned to give me a gift. She had been so bowled over by her reading and by all that I could tell her, that she wanted to show just how much she appreciated it. I never expected it, but gifts are always nice.

Sometimes the healing process can take time. It's not always the case that a reading equals instant closure. Even with something as extraordinary as a message from a loved one who's passed on, it can take time to properly digest the information. I don't always get to see this process, especially when I only visit America once or twice every couple of years. But when I do, it is very special.

A friend of Mary's had booked a private reading, deeply grieving her husband. The only way that I could describe this woman was broken, shattered by her loss. As with every reading, I explained how I worked and possibly what to expect. Her husband came forward.

'He keeps showing me cars, like lots and lots of cars as if they were his whole life.' An understatement as it turned out. He wasn't simply a fan of cars but was part of one of the largest dealerships. This wouldn't be the only, let's call it, misinterpretation of the day. I kept getting the word 'herb' – was he a cook, a gardener, a big fan of parsley?

'No, but his brother's name was Herb or Herbert,' his wife told me. Not exactly a common name in Scotland. Each piece of information she recognised and was able to explain. When I saw police motorbikes along a highway, she part-laughed and part-cried. Her husband had been so well-known and well-loved that the police had to close the highway for the procession. Many people showed up to pay their respects.

Through Spirit, I was able to tell her what she was doing at his bedside when he passed and how he watches over her, making sure she's alright. To borrow an American term, the 'homerun' of the reading was describing how she slept with a piece of her husband's clothing under her pillow every night. No one knew she did this.

'What's this about his favourite candy? It's a chocolate bar with nuts in it, maybe almonds. He's telling me you almost bought some today for him, but changed your mind.'

She gasped and cried, 'His favourite chocolate bar was a Hershey's bar with nuts!'

After the tears, after the reading, she left smiling; she could not stop. This woman had come in broken, devastated, and was leaving smiling from ear to ear. The healing she needed had begun. Every time I visit Boston, she returns for a reading. Each time, she seems happier, lighter, her smile brighter. It's a wonderful chance to see her progress. And she always brings some Hershey's to share.

During that first visit to America, I was reassured that my way of reading would be received well and that my gifts could serve and heal people both here and at home. Grief and mourning, the need to heal, and the curiosity about what happens after death are not limited by country, language or nationality. It is part of what makes us human.

For my second trip, I was based in Maine, at a spiritualist camp called Camp Etna. Yes, they really do have spiritualist camps. It's less friendship-bracelet-making and stories-around-the-campfire, and more learning-to-speak-to-the-dead. Either way, there were still marshmallows.

Camp Etna was hosting an international week. Mediums from all around the globe had been asked to this conference, to host, talk and demonstrate. I was already on my way out to Maine, having a dedicated week booked when my mentor Sandra invited me to come earlier. Sandra was leading this international week and was insistent I come and teach with her. I certainly wasn't going to turn her down.

During my time at camp, I conducted readings, did demonstrations, ran workshops, the whole shebang, helping, encouraging and teaching these mediums how to improve their skills. I introduced my Scottish straight-to-the-point style of reading, which the attendees welcomed. With something like mediumship, especially when it's described as a gift and it 'comes' to you naturally, you wouldn't think there was such a thing as improving on it. The spirits come, talk and you regurgitate. But there are so many ways of hearing and seeing spirits, and of conveying the messages they bring. The workshops I ran were a testament to this. Many of the attendees were working mediums, there to hone their gifts, maybe learn a new skill, it was almost like a spiritual writer's retreat.

It was during one of Sandra's workshops that I met Jeannie. A medium in her own right, Jeannie had heard of me when my name cropped up in conversations during International Week. From the scraps she had heard, she knew she could learn from me. She asked the spirit world for a sign, that if she met me, she would stay for my week. Sure enough, I appeared in Sandra's workshop, totally out of the blue. In Sandra's class of 30, Jeannie took in everything I had to say, enjoyed not only my style but my way of understanding this world and the work we do. Things clicked into place for her, and she saw in my Scottish style what she did and wanted to do. In no time at all, she was signed up for my classes.

When it was my turn to teach, it was wonderful and beautiful to see what Jeannie was already capable of. All I did was help deepen her understanding and introduce her to more effective ways of reading and giving messages. I always said that Jeannie was a diamond in the rough. I was merely adding some polish.

Since then, our relationship has blossomed into a life-long friendship. We have done demonstrations and workshops together, and sometimes we'll just go for lunch. I've helped her set up shows and put together tours, all the back-office minutiae of a working medium. In fact, after my week of teaching, Jeannie wanted to know if I would be back in America as she was dying to host me in her hometown of Brewer, Maine. What was another transatlantic trip?

There in her hometown, it was amazing to do an entire event with Jeannie. Our different styles of mediumship are so complimentary, the two of us sharing the stage and connecting with Spirit together. We worked in such a harmonious way, the audience was incredibly receptive. Different from Scotland, different from England, different even from Camp Etna, I was greeted with a great assortment of peoples and cultures and backgrounds that I'd never read for. But there I was, giving beautiful and important messages in a beautiful venue.

Word-of-mouth had always been my greatest ally; just look at what happened in Campbeltown. America was no different. During my stay with Mary, I was asked by Keith and Dan who run The Harmony Centre in Arizona, to join them. They were taking a risk inviting me out as we had never met. They had only heard of me and my reputation via the great medium grapevine, extending from Camp Etna, Maine all the way to Arizona. They set up readings, workshops and demonstrations for me, and let me get on with it. Hopefully, this leap of faith they took paid off.

Despite several visits, and interactions with all types of Americans, there were still some cultural barriers that I had to cross. With names like Randy and Cindy, I was faced with an unfamiliar language. Perhaps the most apparent one was the sudden presence of guns in my readings. Spirits would come through holding, owning or shooting guns. During a reading at The Harmony Centre, one woman had a man come through carrying an old-fashioned pistol. For a 19-year-old medium from Port Glasgow, this seemed unusual. I soon found out this was pretty normal for Arizona.

It became more challenging and more heart-breaking, even for a medium who works with the dead, when I had to relay how a spirit – someone's wife, someone's grandparent, someone's child – had passed in a shooting. I once read for a couple who had lost their son to suicide. As I was giving the reading, I explained how it seemed like their son's death had 'gone with a bang'. Unknowingly, my hand had moved while I had been talking, forming a gun pointed at my head. The boy had taken his life with a gun. But I had to learn to adapt, to get used to this American normal.

Of course, none of these experiences would have been possible without the supportive actions of Mary – and I don't think she knows just how important she's been to my American journey. She has paved the way for me and opened doors that I don't think I would have been able to find the key for.

It was Mary who introduced me to American medium, John Holland. Yet again, Mary had been singing my praises, talking me and my 'phenomenal' mediumship up to John. So much so that he attended one of my events with a friend. It happened that his friend received a message during the event. Unfortunately, I can't remember the exact details, but it was powerful and beautiful enough to reduce her to tears during the interval. This was clearly a sign for John.

From there, we began to get to know one another. We talked, had dinner, and he invited me to stay with him. We did events and conducted readings together. To use an Americanism I've picked up, Mary hit it out of the park again. Another colleague, another friend, another opportunity.

Visiting America as many times as I have now, I can confirm that I am getting the hang of it. Being able to travel and work in the States has been remarkable. My mind and abilities have been broadened by the diverse, charming and welcoming collection of people I have met and read for. I have allowed my readings and gift to flow, to seize every opportunity I can, and to leave very few stones unturned. Honestly, the trips I have made to

America have made me the medium I am today. Thankfully, the feeling is mutual, the Americans enjoy my no-nonsense style of mediumship, so much so that I am still allowed back.

Every time I go back, I seem to stay a little bit longer. Now at 30, I'm going for 5 months, splitting that between a tour of 3 months and 2 months. And who knows how much more that could grow. I have already gone from Washington to Maine to Arizona, maybe one day I'll be doing readings on a beach in Hawaii in between sips of a Mai Tai. Now, that I could do no problem.

7

Between setting up my own Spiritualist centre, touring and my many other adventures in mediumship, I could finally say, 'Yes, this is it, I am a full-time medium.' Writing for The Sun had sky-rocketed my career, but the tour in America had been a wake-up call. It was the final cog clicking into place. This was no longer a passion project or a pastime; I was no longer speaking once or twice a week in a damp church. This was the life I had chosen. Or perhaps chosen for me, who really knows?

Everything became more professional. I had Mark acting as agent-cum-manager, setting up everything from accounts to hotel arrangements. He did everything but actually speak to the dead. Invoices were sent, bookings organised and appointments with accountants set up. Mum and Gran too became more supportive and receptive to the idea. Who knew telling people your son or grandson is a medium could be such an ice-breaker?

When your child or grandchild realises that they have this amazing gift, one that evolves into an unusual career path, you're bound to have many concerns. This was a silly mistake, they said, leaving the call centre to pursue mediumship. And while I could never undervalue my love for my Gran and Mum, it felt good to show them that it was possible. We all came to understand this was my path and there was no other way.

I had other dreams and aspirations. At five years old, I wasn't telling my teacher that when I grew up, I wanted to stand on a stage and tell strangers about their dead loved ones. But all the other dreams I had, like joining the police force, were banished. I had worked my way through the labyrinth of life and found, like buried treasure, what I was meant to do. New dreams were picked up along the way, some of them realised and others not yet. I had become absorbed into this life as a medium.

To say that I had accepted and fully given myself to this life does not mean I didn't have doubts. Every time I perform or conduct a reading, I am placing myself in a vulnerable position. From a business point of view, I have people purchasing a service i.e. a message from a loved one. And, like waiting for that new shirt you want to be back in stock in your size, I cannot always guarantee that service. I am trusting that people will come to tours and shows and private readings, and pay for them, knowing that they might not receive a message. I could not rely on a couple of readings a week and a Sunday show for 50 people. This was my career now. Thankfully, people responded and audiences continued to grow, into their hundreds.

On the more spiritual side of vulnerability, I was opening myself up to spirits who could have had tragic and traumatic lives, that wanted to deliver messages to reassure their loved ones. Every reading is an emotional rollercoaster and until I begin, I don't know what kind of ride I'm in for. It could be a calm, friendly train, easy and harmonious. The connection is full of loving and soothing words and laughter at almost-forgotten inside jokes. The alternative is your Thorpe Park's Rollercoaster of Doom kind of reading, where I want to scream at the top of my lungs, and cry with fright and pain. It is as unpredictable as it is rewarding.

These are not my feelings, but the spirits'. Every message, image or word that I receive is laden with emotion. We're talking about passed loved ones, people who are grieving, who've suffered traumatic deaths, who have left things unsaid. That's a giant emotional weight to bear for one person. It is exhausting dealing with your own sadness, happiness and fear. Imagine what it's like dealing with a dozen or so spirits' sadness, happiness and fear.

Without sounding like a martyr, it is something I have to live with and work through. I have to separate myself and my internal emotional life from the spirits'. For me, it is a gift. The ability to feel and speak for these spirits, to reunite and reconnect them with their loved ones, is an honour. Honour and gratitude help to alleviate some of the emotional strain. Empathy was part of my DNA long before I was a medium, so I already had the capacity to share others' emotions.

And I never know how I'm going to react, what my state will be when I clamber off the rollercoaster. Sometimes I can leave a reading practically dancing on the ceiling if it went well. Other times, if the message has been challenging or the passing difficult, it takes its toll. I've conducted readings where spirits have passed during 9/11 and I can hear the cries; they are always difficult ones.

All these emotions I deal with during the reading. Between myself and my client, we deal with them there and then, whether it's crying, laughing or a little of both. I want to make sure the client leaves the reading with happy memories and messages, treasuring them and replacing the negative emotions. I reassure my clients, and myself, that the hurt and the trauma, the physical death, was only a snapshot of that person's life. Through my mediumship, a whole life is explored, a life that continues and I can evidence after death. That is the thought I want clients to take home with them.

Thanks to word of mouth, audiences continued to grow. Whenever I go back to America, more shows are booked and more seats are squeezed into halls and churches. While I don't like to say it, the more bums on seats, the greater the boost for me. It's not an ego boost, I don't need that, but a boost to my self-belief. If people from a whole different continent believe in me, if people I have never met trust that I can make these connections, I should believe in myself.

Spirit might always have my back, teaching and guiding me, and I have faith in Spirit, but that does not mean mediumship is without obstacles. As my sight progressively deteriorated, I could no longer work in the same way. Usually, I would stand and look out at the audience, allowing spirits to visually guide me to the loved one they wanted to connect to. I would give details and evidence, names and relationships, and people would wave or stand up, claiming the message for themselves. I could see and shout for the man in the white shirt or the woman in the green dress, yes, this is for you.

Now, even if they are only a few rows back, I'm not going to see them. While my gift had never faltered, my confidence in my ability did. How could I stand up in front of an audience, an audience I could barely see, and deliver these messages? For a while, each time I took to the stage, I would wonder, 'Is this it? Is this the time I fall flat on my face?'

But just as there are guide dogs for the blind, hearing aids for the deaf and blue badges for parking, Spirit was able to help me adapt my gift, making it more disabled-user friendly. When I began as a medium, I primarily worked visually, using clairvoyance, 'clear seeing' and spirits would provide images for me to interpret, turning them into messages, kind of like translating hieroglyphs or emojis into words. As the medium, it was up to me to try and understand what any image meant, turning a string of pictures into a story that someone might recognise.

With my physical sight worsening, I had to go away and figure out how I should be working. Was there a better way for me? The process was made more challenging by the physical obstacles I was dealing with, the tests, the diagnoses and the subsequent depression.

As I began to see a way through the depression, I gained a sense that there was something else, something better on the other side for me. Okay, I had a silent cry but then I turned to my dad begging for his help, asking him to help me receive clearer messages and information via clairaudience, 'clear listening', to become more accurate, more powerful, anything to help me. There is a poetically devastating symmetry to it. When I began losing my physical sight, I developed a second sight. As my physical sight worsened, my other physical senses picked up the slack. My other spiritual senses did the same.

The shift to a greater reliance on clairaudience was by no means instant. I took longer pauses when performing, waiting for a voice to become clearer or repeat a name I had missed. After a few tries, subtle whispers began. Every hair on my ears would stand on end, like the gathering of static. The more voices I heard, the easier it was for me to tune into them, to lean into my spiritual hearing. All the noise and chatter in the present, in the physical, I learnt to filter out. With practice, the voices became clearer. Practising this during one-to-one readings was invaluable, having the luxury to really listen to the voices of spirits. I would hear names and details. Coming from the (dead) horse's mouth, spelled more accurate readings.

When working clairvoyantly, I was having to rely on seeing and knowing. Being shown an image of a teddy bear for example, I had to trust in my interpretation that this was the first present someone's dad ever gave them.

The details were greater and more accurate with clairaudience; I was being told the information as if the spirit was standing over my shoulder. I wasn't seeing a male spirit and waiting to figure out whether it was a brother, father or grandfather, the spirit was giving me these details verbally. I knew from the outset that I was talking to a grandfather.

I also became aware of information that I could only relay through clairaudience. No matter how clear the image, how powerful the spirit or how effective the medium is, it is easier to give details through clairaudience. How they spoke, accents and idiosyncrasies, lisps and stutters, are better understood from listening rather than seeing. The evidence I was now able to give was startling, touching on things that I had not, nor could not before. Just as the spirits were trying to be more specific, I was trying to replicate this for my audiences.

There have been, and continue to be, instances where using clairaudience has been not only helpful but a blessing. Some messages are best communicated through one's voice. A husband and wife came to one of my shows in Greenock, and their son who had passed made himself known. He was able to tell me exactly what had happened to him and gave his parents the answers they needed. The night he'd passed, he had tried to call an ambulance. Through the direct details, I was able to communicate that he had choked. He knew about the inquest following his death. 'There was more someone could've done,' he told me, and I told his parents, 'Someone didn't do something.' When the bodycam footage was seen, it came to light that the police had not attempted CPR.

There was no way I could have been so direct and specific with clairvoyance. The son might have shown me a police car or made me feel the choking and see him on the ground. But with the spirit narrating the scene like a spectral audiobook, those details became crystal clear. It's like being a voiceover actor dubbing a foreign film. I have to tune into the language of the spirits, a language that isn't always clear or consistent with 'living' language, and then present this to an audience. There is an added power to that clarity, that I am speaking, not just seeing spirits, that can make doubts disappear.

I was able to introduce language, the way families speak to each other, into my readings. Every place I have performed, I will come across words and have no idea what the spirit is on about. During a reading in Inverness, I kept talking about a wagon and had no clue what it meant. But to the audience, to the loved one whose connection it was, it made perfect sense. For future reference, a wagon is a van in Inverness; who knew?

Of course, the further afield I travelled, the greater the variety of languages I came across via Spirit. In America especially, I was using words that I would never use, trusting Spirit as well as the audience. It was firehouse rather than fire station, state trooper or cop versus police officer.

The depth of details that clairaudience can provide goes beyond local words and slang. During a couple of demonstrations, I have heard complete languages that I can't identify. Thankfully, I do not thrash around the stage speaking in tongues when this happens. All I can do is try to repeat it the way I've heard it. Really, I could do with spirits sounding it out. In Colchester and Hamilton, I've had to give names, use sounds and articulations that were alien to me.

In Colchester, a black couple in Spirit came forward for a couple in the audience. I gave them all the evidence I could, that they were from Ghana, but the name was a little stuck in translation. It was a name from a language, from a country and from a spirit, that I didn't know. In Hamilton, I was able to give a woman her mother's name… in Chinese!

I wouldn't know Chinese, how it sounds or how to speak it, if it bit me on the nose. But with these experiences with spirits and the plethora of languages they speak, I've had to learn to keep my mind, and my mouth, open. Even if I have to sound it out like a children's TV presenter, someone will recognise what I'm saying. I'm waiting for the day a spirit has me speaking Elvish or Klingon.

I was able to pick up ideas about the spirits' personalities from how they spoke too, ideas that couldn't be communicated before. Some spoke gently and I would have to lean in a little, like trying to hear someone in a crowded bar. Others were loud and boisterous, and I felt their excitement myself. Some spoke so fast that I would have to ask them to slow down. 'Sorry, was that Harry or Barry?'

Some spirits attempted to play the comedian, cheeky chaps and lasses in life and Spirit. I have to tread carefully when I get whispered expletives and innuendos in my ear. Why they can't just say I'm okay over here, I don't know.

Once, in The Gamble Halls in Gourock, a male spirit could not wait to tell me about a running joke that he was, in his words, 'hung like a horse'. How do you say that to a room full of strangers, expecting some respect, only for this 20-something-year-old to swagger on and talk about a well-endowed spirit?

'Would you understand a standing joke about him being the big man, or people thinking…'

'Yes, I know exactly what you mean,' said the woman with whom I'd connected. I didn't need to say any more.

While it might be a laugh to get these messages, I have learnt to judge my audiences, whether they're more reserved or more jovial. I can then make decisions about how messages are relayed. Am I going in word-for-word or do I need to be delicate? During a reconnection in Elgin, a spirit came forward for his mother, giving me his name, her name and how he died. He told me that he had committed suicide by gassing himself in his car. I told his mother that he had taken his own life and that there was a car involved. That's all she needed to know, that was all anyone needed to know.

Part of what I do as a medium is to consider both the spirits' and their living relatives' dignity. I am not in the business of being scandalous. I have enough faith in my gift that I don't need to stroke my ego by exposing the spirit's or relative's life. I have to work subtly without being obscure or seeming unsure. I pass on the messages of Spirit, in which there can be intimate details. Nobody but the spirit and the family connection need to know the nitty-gritty. My own words have to do then.

In a private reading, the issue of possibly airing dirty laundry is lessened. I have the luxury of time, taking my client by the hand. I am better able to relay the spirit's message as it's spoken when it's less of a spectator sport. Personal information, whether upsetting or jovial, can be more direct and I don't need to monitor what I say as much.

Readings can grow and develop better then and I like to describe them as onions, with many layers to unravel. The client, the spirit and I agreeing on what could happen and be said can go deeper into the reading. Like a spiral falling inwards, the spirit's words I speak become more detailed. Like shifting the lens on a microscope, any images I see come into focus.

A reading I conducted in America exemplifies this onion-like unravelling. When I first begin a private session, I will often draw and doodle on a blank pad; it helps centre and prepare me, and words sometimes appear. During this reading, as the client entered, I wrote the word 'balloons'. I thought nothing of it and began the reading. The woman's husband insisted that I told her, 'You and I will always be stuck together.' He also showed me an image of Central Park.

On her husband's anniversary, she and her son released balloons over Central Park, including a foil heart, and a foil 'I' and 'You'. As they sailed across the park, the 'I' and 'You' became tangled in a tree. 'You' and 'I' were stuck together. For two weeks they were in that tree until a friend collected them. Now the woman has them framed in her home.

By openly saying what the spirit had told me, by explaining the images I had seen, by writing 'balloons' on my pad, the reading deepened and the message was clarified. It was not my job to interpret what the spirit was saying, only that I said it. Trying to unpick the little idioms and sayings that exist between families could have been futile. Sometimes, loved ones only need to hear the words. The wonders of clairaudience.

As I have grown into my clairaudience, I've appreciated that I'm in this beautiful place where my readings have become more conversational. I'm a middle man, an interpreter between Spirit and loved ones, and the messages need to be direct sometimes. When I tell a client that her father's spirit is helping heal her brother's addiction, it means that little bit more when I'm being told this directly. It might be my mouth moving, but it's the spirit's words.

And that feels great, that added precision. I have had clients ask specific questions and I'm able to relay accurate answers from the spirit talking to me. If I could have done that during school tests, I would've been top of the class. At the end of a reading in Helensburgh, I asked my client whether she had any questions for her father. She wanted to know where the key was. Almost immediately, I heard her father tell me that it was in the garage, in the box beside the wireless. Later on, I received a message from this woman, and lo and behold, the missing key was in the box beside the wireless, in the garage. As I end up saying at most of my shows, you couldn't make it up.

I have by no means completely mastered clairaudience yet. At first, it took me a year or so to become comfortable with it. With all the practice and work I had put in, I grew from a vulnerable insecure Dominic, anxious that my disability could bring a halt to my path, to a more confident Dominic. I do address it at my shows as a little disclaimer, 'If you think the message is for you, do not sit there waving your hands because I am not going to see you. You're gonna have to speak up.'

With the additional clairaudience, I began to have new mediumistic experiences. Sometimes it can feel like trying to wrangle a classroom of unruly children, several voices all at once and none of them clear. Once, I was demonstrating when a father figure called David wanted to communicate with me; he had died from a heart attack and wanted to talk to his daughter-in-law, sitting to my left.

What was bizarre was that two other women in the audience also recognised their fathers from my description. One lady withdrew once I'd given the age range of the father. But the other lady could still understand the evidence: the age range, the personality, the issues with alcohol. Suddenly, I was Solomon trying to decide which mother should keep the baby.

I asked Spirit how I should deal with this; was there a 'correct' spirit and would I have to ask them to take it in turns? The first spirit approached me to say that he wanted to speak to the first lady. I made the connection and delivered the message before moving on to the second lady. The second lady's message became clearer as I went on, with her late grandmother adding her own message.

I learnt that this phenomenon, this piggy-backing, is not uncommon. Even as we can be timid or shy in life, spirits can be too. Plus, the time to convey a message is limited. Sometimes they need a little push or an introduction from another spirit. To strengthen their presence, to make themselves heard, spirits will look for similarities, names, how they passed and who they want to talk to.

With enough in common, they make their voices louder, working together, and I can hardly tune them out. Otherwise, I have to call on my dad to escort one spirit into the wings, a spiritual green room if you will, while I complete the first connection. Two similar spirits can come through, with enough in common to make two totally different connections.

Between spirits grappling for attention, spiritually shouting my name, and some coupling up, I've found that I have to 'disappear' more with clairaudience. There is no puff of smoke while I vanish behind a curtain, but I have to place my mind on pause. When working clairvoyantly, my mind is always ticking away. I have got to decode what these images mean, and what message can be understood in these pictures. With clairaudience, I am speaking the words I am given.

In some ways, I become an empty vessel; the spirits pour their messages into me and I serve them to their loved ones. But if my head is brimming over with me, those important words might not find their way out. I refer to this as sinking or pushing my mind to the side. Before I begin, I'll be backstage and building this energy by hyping myself up. When I first address the audience, this energy steers me into a hypnotic state. I can settle myself, push my mind to the side and that is when I become aware of Spirit. And that's it. Despite the stereotype of mediumship, the very idea of spirit communication, it is not all mystical song-and-dance; I can't even meditate. Sure, I will set my intention and might say a wee prayer, but that is as ritualised as it gets.

A medium, in my humble opinion, never stops developing. Pushed to do so, my mediumship has evolved and kept pace alongside my life. Gaining and developing clairaudience was a blessing and gave me the confidence I needed when I needed it. It has come with its own perks and pitfalls, but I like to think it's made me a better medium, more accurate, precise and detailed. While I continued to work this way, I could also turn my mind to other pursuits.

8

When people begin to explore Spiritualism, either in its entirety or just mediumship, there is some unlearning to do. Having read for many and travelled far, I have heard the whole spectrum of myths and misconceptions. If people's first, and sometimes only, experience of spirits and mediumship is from Derek Acorah 'talking' to a Victorian child while Yvette Fielding's swearing is bleeped, they'll be some misunderstandings.

How do you do it? Is it safe? Isn't it bad? Is there someone here now? Funnily enough, speaking to the dead does not come with its own FAQs.

One of the most common questions is, are spirits everywhere? The minute people discover I'm a medium, after overcoming the shock, suspicion and scepticism, their eyes start darting around. For whatever reason, people think that spirits are following them, sometimes to places, let's just say, you would not want a spirit to follow you. If I had a pound for every time someone asked me if their dead grandparent follows them to the toilet, I could quit my job and settle down on an island beach.

One of the beliefs that I talk about, that I have evidence for, is that spirits continue to live on. It might not be in a way we can see or understand, and we might not be able to interact with them in the same way. But they are present. When I do a reading or a show, both the audience and I are creating a space to allow for that spirit contact. I am putting the proverbial open sign on the door of the space. Together, we say, 'Come on in.'

When I make a connection, the spirit gives me information about the receiver's past and their shared memories. This only evidences that I am speaking with the spirit. The information I receive about the present and things that have happened after the spirit's death, prove that the spirit lives on. And no one, dead or alive, is following you to the loo.

When I was still a young developing medium at the Butterfly Fellowship, I delivered a message to a lady from her father. Clairvoyantly, I saw a rubbish bin. There was no bin bag in it, but there was a mouse. (For the record, this is not the weirdest message I have given.)

'Your dad is showing me a bin inside your house, but it has a mouse in it,' I said.

'Definitely not!'

To be honest, I would also be confused and maybe a little offended if someone told me there was a mouse in my house, especially, if that person claimed to be speaking to my dead dad. But I told her that this is what her dad was showing me and to check the bin when she got home.

The following week, she came back to the church, excited and desperate to show me something. She pulled up a photo on her phone. After her reading, she had gone home and checked her bin. As advised, or predicted, there was a mouse.

Of all the messages a loved one could pass on, the reassurances that they are okay, the thanks for being cared for, why did this woman's father show me a dead mouse? The woman herself had the answer. The message (and the mouse) proved to her that her father was very much around her.

It takes great confidence for a medium to offer statements and interpret clairvoyant images when they seem trivial or downright bizarre. I am not able to control what a spirit shows or tells me, all I can control is how I give that message. Some messages and images are complicated, tricky or, like the mouse, appear nonsensical. But my conviction and trust in Spirit is that I am being shown it for a reason.

These odd images, messages thrown out like confetti, could make easy fodder for sceptics. They seem random, plucked out of my own imagination rather than spiritual messages. It is not about proving people wrong, embarrassing them or myself. With the lady and the mouse, she could have chosen not to say anything. Her pride might've been wounded or she might've been embarrassed. And I would never have known the end of the story. But she did come back. As I had given her evidence of my speaking with her dad, she gave me evidence that I had seen correctly. Not only that, but it is a sensational confidence boost when someone says to me, 'That made no sense at the time, but you were right.'

We can see this all the time around us. People often talk about seeing robins or white feathers or specific numbers. These are signs sent from their loved ones in Spirit. Spirits have to get inventive if they want our attention. Feathers and numbers are like a code and mediums are the code-breakers. Our loved ones do not pass over or move out of our lives when they die. They are right next to us.

This is one of the main differences between what I do, Spiritualism, and other mainstream religions. And these differences can sometimes make people wary. Over the years I have been asked about where, how and if religion is compatible with mediumship. On the surface, it can seem… ungodly. In the numerous faiths of the world, the teachings about death are clear. When we die, our spirits travel from the material world to an afterlife: Heaven, Hell, Paradise, Swarg (Hindu afterlife), or an Otherworld. What I can do contradicts this very idea.

So many religions have their beliefs and rites focused on death and an afterlife. For little old Port Glasgow-born speaking-to-the-dead me to come on along and say, 'That's not quite right,' you're going to get some funny looks. The difference is I have proof. It is not just myself who is able to prove it, but Spiritualism as a path is based on evidence. Other religions are based on faith and belief, something non-material, ethereal and transcendent. Spiritualism is about proof and tangible evidence.

You could debate all day about the existence of a god. You can spend day after day praying. Both these things rely on belief, that you believe in God and believe that your prayers are heard. When you come to a Spiritualist Church, you do not need to believe it. You know, the medium knows and the spirit knows exactly the last present your mum gave you, right down to what it looks like and where you currently keep it. It's less 'when you're dead, you're dead' and more 'they're still with us.'

Disclaimer: this is not some evangelical Bat Signal to abandon your religion and find your closest Spiritualist church, to wait patiently for your grandad to tell you if you'll pass your driving test. Nor am I saying that what I do is better than other religions. It is a neutral objective account of the differences I have experienced.

Some people, some mediums, do meld their mediumship with their personal spiritual beliefs. The gift of mediumship could be a gift from God. They might talk about Heaven, even angels. But Spiritualism is separate from this; there's no dogma, no judgement, no sense of superiority or my-faith-is-the-right-faith. It focuses on evidence, turning belief into knowledge, and healing.

Even if someone doesn't come from a religious background, I try to share as much as I know about spirits as I can, to dismiss certain cultural preconceived ideas. Some of them are pretty minor misinterpretations. For example, I am often asked about ghosts; do they exist, have I seen one etc.? I don't deal with ghosts; hypocritical for someone who speaks to the dead, but spirits and ghosts are not the same.

Linguistically we might use them interchangeably, but spiritually they are apples and oranges.

For me, spirits are still alive in a way, they have a consciousness and can interact with people. Ghosts on the other hand are the opposite. They are more like impressions, energies that are left behind in a particular place for example. My preferred analogy is, if a spirit is the finger, able to point and press and click, then a ghost is the fingerprint, something left behind, but can be 'read'. A psychic might read these impressions like following a ghostly breadcrumb path, whereas a medium will talk directly to the source.

Just as spirits continue to live, it is important to understand how they live. Honestly, other than the non-material aspect, spirits are mostly the same as they were when alive. If they suffered from an illness or long-term disease, they might show or tell me what it was and where on the body it affected them. They don't carry that disease into Spirit, but all the other parts of life, thinking, feeling, and certain senses, all continue. Understanding this opens up how we think of spirits, especially when it comes to mediumship.

Why might a spirit want to make contact? I am rarely asked to give dire warnings or reveal where the family gold is. As flesh-and-blood people, those who receive messages, it's easy to forget that the spirits of our loved ones are also mourning. They are in the same boat as we are, separate from and unable to communicate with our families. Both sides need communication and healing, comfort and love. Just as the living need reassurance that the dead are at peace, that they are no longer in pain, the dead want to make sure the living are still- well, living.

The messages I deliver from spirits are about healing and attempting to soothe broken hearts. Hopefully, I can help heal both the living recipient and their passed loved one. More than that, messages can inspire and motivate people, encouraging them to pick up the pieces of their lives, inspired by their spirit-given knowledge.

At a show in Ayr, I was approached by a woman in Spirit. Without sounding too corny or coarse, the only way to describe this woman was that she was a dead ringer for everyone's favourite soap opera landlady, Peggy Mitchell as portrayed by Barbara Windsor. I was told that she had only passed recently, that she was a mother and grandmother, looking to connect with her daughter and granddaughter. More details were shared and I gestured to the area of the audience the spirit guided me.

Once I had found the mother and daughter duo, I began to receive details clairaudiently.

'Son, I'm not registered as dead,' the spirit told me.

'You're having a laugh,' I retorted.

'Go one,' she urged, 'ask them.'

I told the mother and daughter what the spirit had told me. Cue them both bursting into tears. Not only had the woman passed recently, but she had passed the night before my show. She showed me relevant papers; the mother did the same, reaching into her bag for the death certificate, an omission that needed to be fixed before the death could be correctly registered. Mother and daughter, on hearing the message from their mother/grandmother, were not only comforted by her continuing presence but were able to honour and remember her the way she wanted. How many of us can say that?

'Well, she wants me to help you plan her funeral,' I told them. Through me, she chose all the details, from the flowers, right down to the date. Of course, her wishes were followed.

Our loved ones do not disappear when we die. Their emotions and bonds, their grief and their heartaches, keep them around their living loved ones. When I conduct a reading, these spirits are invited to help us cope with the loss. As living family and friends, they wouldn't abandon us. It is no different in Spirit, they never want to wander far from us.

To continue this idea of spirits continuing to live, spirits can evolve. I'm not talking about Pokémon, spirits becoming something else. But like the living, they have to grow and evolve emotionally. They learn to forgive and apologise and appreciate what is and what is not important.

Superficially, for my sake at least, they also have to keep their references up to date. When working clairaudiently, the words don't need changing or explaining. Yes, there have been times when spirits have used slang words or terms specific to areas. But when I work clairvoyantly, even if the image requires some explaining, I still need to at least be able to recognise it.

During a Facebook Live, where viewers can send in their questions or names of loved ones, a man asked about his daughter. Immediately, I became aware of her approaching me. As I was passing information from his daughter, I was shown a very random image. The spirit showed me a bottle of Britney Spears perfume! This could have meant anything, from the girl liking the perfume to her dad buying it for her.

Doing my best to make sense of it, I added that his daughter must have liked Britney Spears and I felt that he treasured this perfume bottle. As it turns out, his daughter's name was Britney and he did still keep the bottle, the one he bought her before her passing. Through a screen, on opposite ends of the world, Spirit was still able to intervene and comfort this dad, via a perfume bottle of all things!

What can surprise people about mediumship and the spirit world is the depth both spirits and mediums can go, into memories, into their lives, but also their emotions. Spirit is very aware of the needs of a sitter; something all mediums should be aware of too. A medium should understand a sitter's emotional needs, and how a reading will impact them, before starting.

It's easy to get carried away in a reading or a demonstration. For the medium, you can be on a roll, dishing out detail after detail. For a sitter, they can want more information, more proof, waiting for the next taste of spiritual comfort. But how this information is communicated needs to be done with the sitter's best interests and emotional well-being in mind.

Sometimes, it is not always the right time. You would think a spirit would be eager to communicate, and they are, but timing is everything. An in-depth reading with a parent who recently lost a child, every emotion still raw, might not be helpful. Emotions can run high and the pain too fresh for both sitter and spirit. A reading should help people to cope with and begin healing from loss, not overwhelm them.

During one reading for a mother who had lost her son, my dad intervened. He explained that the boy wouldn't be able to communicate well because his grief was still too strong. Perhaps not the message the mother wanted to hear, but it was enough for her. Rather than memories, the boy shared present information with me: what was happening in his mother's life, his family and his passing. The mother, naturally, wanted more. We compromised and I invited her to return in six months.

When she left, I asked my father why I wasn't able to conduct a full reading with her son. He explained that if her son had revisited every detail of their past, the life they had and could have had together, it would have made the grieving process harder. People need time to understand and accept that their loved one's physical earthly life has ended before introducing a continued spiritual life.

Don't think that I am cruelly starving clients of evidence and possibly important healing messages. Having suffered grief myself, I understand the importance of going through the emotions first.

When you're working as a medium, occasionally you come with odd esoteric accoutrements such as tarot cards. People see these and jump to certain conclusions. More often than not these conclusions, and the questions they ask me, are about seeing the future.

Unfortunately, mediumship is not fortune-telling or prophesying. I am not the Oracle of Delphi nor Mystic Meg. Sometimes, I will have messages from Spirit that sound predictive. They might tell me about a project you're undertaking and will succeed at, or a situation that will eventually go your way. It might sound like forecasting, but it's really nothing more than a very good hunch.

As humans, we tend to conflate information from an unknown or unseeable source as mystical or true. In the same way that spirits continue to live, they still have certain human limitations. They cannot see the future, for the future is not set in stone. When we pass, there is not a magical moment of enlightenment, of ultimate clarity that includes the future. The way I see and talk about it, spirits can just see more, their sight is a little clearer than our physical one.

When I had the centre in West Blackhall Street, a woman came in for a reading. I asked her what kind of reading she wanted, one to give her guidance about her life or one from a spirit. She chose a medium-based reading and so I began. A gentleman approached me and told me he was her father. I gave her all the evidential proof I usually would, as passed to me by her spirit father. What was odd was the woman had believed her father was still alive.

Even mediums have to double-check sometimes. But no, I checked in with the spirit, making sure I got his name, age and home town correct, and I had. This was the woman's father who had passed away. The woman told me she hadn't had any contact with her father for several years. The memories I was able to relay, she confirmed were accurate.

After the reading, I asked her to go and find out what had happened to her father. Everything else Spirit gave me was correct and she confirmed it, but I wanted to make sure. That night, I wracked my brain wondering what had happened and whether I had done the right thing by telling her. No one can imagine being told a loved one has passed in such a way. I couldn't have imagined delivering that news. 99% of the readings I give, the recipient knows the individual has passed. That's why people come to me!

Maybe I was having an off day and misinterpreted who the spirit was. Father could have been Grandfather or maybe a father figure. Maybe my gift was on the fritz. Spirit assured me however that I had been correct, that it was a privilege that I was able to reconnect father and daughter after so many years.

The following day, the woman sent me a message. After the reading, she found out that her father had indeed passed away, but no one on her side of the family had been informed. I won't lie and say I didn't breathe a small sigh of relief, despite also feeling heart-sick for the woman. But through Spirit, she was given this vital piece of knowledge. It wasn't foresight or fortune-telling, and I was not reading omens of death from leaves in a teacup. Spirit could just see more, like looking at the whole picture rather than one corner of it. And when we have not seen it yet, it looks more like foretelling than it actually is.

Mediumship is not as magical, mystical or mysterious as it appears. That's just how it looks on the telly. After all, for me, it is very every day. We all have to unlearn and re-evaluate our beliefs when we come in contact with mediumship and Spiritualism. I had to do the same at the beginning of my journey. But the benefits that can be reaped, the healing, the comfort are worth that little bit of questioning. When you've answered the same questions as I have and put to bed as many misconceptions as I have, you realise you've built up quite the knowledge. Enough knowledge to start passing it on to others.

9

What's a guy to do, having developed his mediumship and learnt a cornucopia of skills? The answer is to teach. This was not a case of 'those who can't do, teach', but rather those who *can* do should teach others. I had been a pupil for years at this point; at churches and centres, practising my abilities. Through Spirit, through my dad, I had been taught skills and ways to develop and deepen my connections. Many of them felt personalised, this was a way I could work that I hadn't seen others use. As these skills had been passed to me, it was only right that I should teach them to other mediums.

At first, there was no arrow pointing me in the direction of teaching. Rather, it was by earthly necessity with maybe a pinch of that divine timing. When Sandra left the Butterfly Centre to work in America, it turned out I was heir presumptive to lead the circle. Already Vice President, it fell to me to become the circle leader, to help attendees develop their skills.

For the students, they were still at the beginning of their journey. I had to start from the basics, drawing on the skills I had been taught and my experiences. We focused on tools, anything from flowers to ribbons. Theoretically, if they could be distracted physically, then their spiritual senses would be open to communication. Creating a foundation is always my first step with student mediums. Once you are on solid spiritual ground, you can progress and personalise. You outgrow flowers and ribbons and you can tune in to Spirit seamlessly. But I wanted to, needed to, teach walking before running.

Very quickly, I began to feel passionate about teaching, taking these students under my wing and sharing everything that I knew. What I was teaching was not from any book or website. Not only had I done the work in circle myself, with other mediums, but had received skills and 'tech' from Spirit. The way I conducted readings felt very personalised, with Spirit stepping in and helping me adapt. These adaptions helped me become a better medium and I wanted to do the same for others. I could tell that they had their own lives, their own things going on. I had to lean into this teaching part of myself, a learned and empathetic Dominic, to ignite their gifts.

But Dominic, I hear you cry, surely mediums are born not made? You said that your dad visited you and from there, you began as a medium. And with plenty of study and learning too, I might add. I might believe that mediums are born and that certain people are predisposed to psychic gifts and medium skills, but that doesn't mean they don't need to train. Harry Potter might have been born a wizard, but without Hogwarts, where would he be?

And like wizards, though with a little less hocus pocus, not everyone can be a medium. As ironic as it sounds, the best mediums are those who do not want to be a medium. Someone who doesn't want this supposed power, glory or even money they assume comes with mediumship. If you had seen some of the hotels I've had to stay in, not a chance.

I am a true believer that you can never completely appreciate the gift of mediumship and become a good medium if you have not been closely affected by death. I've seen so many times that individuals who have been touched by Spirit are those who have experienced some type of trauma. This trauma often provides the trigger for this gift awakening in the individual's soul. Think of Matilda: the abuse from her parents and Miss Trunchbull triggered her powers. Though making myself a bowl of cereal with telekinesis is a little beyond me. You would need to find a different teacher for that.

A good medium must be authentic, without expectations or agenda. Being a medium can throw curveballs into your life, and you have to be ready, willing even, to accept that and dedicate your life to it. For me, it's not a hobby or a skill or simply a job, but a whole lifestyle. There are few careers that totally and completely become your life. You have to give yourself 100% to Spirit and all those people you are going help.

I've realised that I have sacrificed plenty of myself, for Dominic-the-medium. Along the way, I have missed birthdays, weddings and a whole host of other occasions to follow this life. And the sacrifices and selflessness are for a lifetime. Recently, at a demonstration in Stoke, I had just about lost my voice. I had two choices: to bow out and get myself better, or to throw myself into it, to try as best I could, to make connections for the audience. Of course, I chose the latter, but this is exemplary of the selflessness required. There can be physical, emotional and spiritual weights to bear. And not everyone can or should do this.

Some have a natural penchant for this way of life, these gifts. There are innumerable mediums and psychics, reminiscing about their childhood imaginary friend who ended up being the spirit of a Victorian child. I am sure this happens, but not every inkling or predisposition is as manifest. Other times, psychics and mediums can influence this cliché. They declare that you've been touched by Spirit or 'you've got *something*' when all you've done is bought some crystals and peed yourself doing a Ouija board.

If an individual does have a medium leaning, this can be read in their aura. You can even tell how these gifts might manifest and in what area their gifts might be. An individual's possible mediumship abilities can also be discovered in a 'soul plan' reading. The idea is a psychic or medium can connect to someone, soul to soul and reveal hidden unconscious truths. I believe only someone with mediumship in their soul, their spiritual DNA, is able to become a medium. Gifts may lie like embers, but they need to be fanned and nurtured through teaching. But that initial spark is essential and innate. Once this is identified, a teacher can decide whether they have the ability to nurture these gifts.

Even if someone were to approach me for teaching, and they had an interest in mediumship, it does not mean that a) they're going to be a medium, or b) become a ground-breaking world-touring medium. It can become a very manufactured almost forced path, between having the faintest of interests and being 'chosen'. A good teacher won't shy aware from saying this.

I have been to circles and churches where people come just for the community. After all, most of these people are mourning, dealing with recent and long-term grief. It is only natural to want to be around people and in spaces that can understand not only what you're going through, but also what you are looking for spiritually.

Just as there are some people born to be mediums, there are also people definitely born not to be. Traits-wise, this would be anybody who lacks ethics, compassion or a filter. No matter how spiritual you are, if you do not know or care how you talk to a grieving child, mother or father, then you have no business being a medium.

I am always cautious about encouraging or mentoring people who have a history of mental health. Becoming a medium means taking on a lot of emotional and mental responsibility. Day-to-day, you are never dealing with just your own emotions. You are an emotional and spiritual crossroads for whole families. If you are unable to process that, to know how to be healthy within yourself, you do not need the extra weight of being a medium.

There can sometimes be a danger risk. As a medium, especially thinking about clairaudience, you have to be discerning. Is this my voice or a spirit's? Is this my imagination or a spirit? Again, if you are unable to differentiate, and if being unable presents a risk, this is not a suitable path for you.

The only other reason that I would not take on a prospective medium is if they're already learning from another teacher. It isn't a pride thing or anything like that. The student needs (and hopefully wants) the best tutelage they can get. Switching between two teachers, who teach and also work very differently, is not going to produce the best results. I always say go and finish that programme first. I don't want to step on anyone's toes and potentially undo their work.

The more I taught and the more that people talked about my teaching, the greater the number of people and churches that began to approach me, inviting me to lead circles and to teach. Every time I led a circle and advised on how best to conduct readings, I would learn too. While I had amassed a back catalogue if you will of mediumship skills, I am not the font of all knowledge. Students would quiz me on how best to do this or that. At first, I wouldn't know, it might be something I hadn't come across before. But I was able to check in with Spirit and get the answers from the source so to speak. Once I had the answer, I could pass it on. Even when it comes to speaking with the dead, you never stop learning.

Slowly, I began to formalise courses for students. I collected and calibrated all they needed to know: the theory, the practice and the exercises. Some of this was for private readings, others for larger demonstrations. My teachings and my roster of students continued to grow. Similar to audience members confirming details during a demonstration, it was a boost to know I was doing something right and that my methods were helping other mediums.

As with my mediumship, the more I taught, the more I understood how I wanted to teach. My teaching ethos was to strip everything back. Whether students were new to mediumship or old mediums looking to learn new tricks, I wanted to get away from the crap. I had always approached mediumship naturally and I wanted to convey this in my teaching. Keeping my approach as organic as possible was what seemed to attract people.

There were no bells and whistles, things they might have seen on TV or at other churches. There would be no need for meditating, wafting burning sage around your body, or opening your chakras. That New Age stuff might work for some, but not me. I wanted all my methods and knowledge to be tried and tested.

The demand for teaching continued to grow, and I began private one-on-one mentoring. Mediums would approach me, looking for intensive training, a year or so of full mediumship immersion. This was aimed more towards mediums who wanted to hone their skills and become better mediums. And I was more than happy to take them on when I could. Because of this, I began to develop whole mentoring programs, sharing and travelling around Scotland. When I had my own centre,

I continued to do my fair share of teaching. Sometimes, I could have between 20 and 30 people, some of who had travelled from various churches to sit in a circle and learn from me.

My real passion is teaching advanced mediums, helping people already on the path and refining their abilities so they can do healing work. Both the mediums and I get more out of this. I get to see what they can do and how they work. From there, I can begin to pare back their approach and judge which things to keep and which to bin, like a spiritual Marie Kondo. Once we arrive at the bare bones, I can begin to help nurture the medium and furnish them with more effective methods.

Part of this stripping back is to deprogram ideas about mediumship and the point of it. The core of my mediumship has always been to heal. In part, this healing comes from learning that life continues. A lot of students' mediumship is evidence-based only. Some mediums can get a name and snippets of information but don't know where to go next.

While I will always begin with evidence and teach the reasoning for doing this, my methods expand on it. One way I do this and teach it is by working with five pieces of evidence. Once you have these, the story unfolds. My readings become conversations, the passing to and fro of healing messages.

This can be a hard pattern to break for some students. Those who have come from a church background and who have been trained a certain way can struggle to move away. Their readings can be proof after proof after proof; reeling off every detail of a dead loved one's life, down to how they liked their tea, might prove something, but it's not exactly healing. I teach them to do more than throw a name out and hope someone says, 'Yes, that's me.' I teach them to say, 'You have an Uncle Patrick.'

Part of my curriculum is focused on using that initial evidence. Some mediums focus on the emotional evidence: 'Your mum thanks you for loving her… your uncle was a happy man.' This is all well and good, but it is not practical evidence. Anyone can say so-and-so was a happy person. The idea is then taking it further, making it more factual. 'Your mum thanks you for loving her,' becomes, 'Your mum thanks you for loving her through her addiction.' More factual, less vague and emotion-based.

While stripping back might be the backbone of my teaching, the heart of it is understanding the bigger picture of mediumship. In my opinion, that is to heal via proof that life goes on and that loved ones are still part of your life.

In private readings, you are given this space to really communicate with and heal people. People don't come to readings or demonstrations simply to know that a medium is legit. And spirits don't appear asking to be proven. People come to know that there is life after our physical death and that their loved ones are still present. Giving only evidence that you're talking to great Aunt Muriel soon becomes flogging a dead horse. We get it, she's here and you're talking to her but where does the reading, where does the medium's message, go from there?

At the end of one reading, I told a woman that her husband has his motor home and is doing Route 66 in the spirit world. Through tears, she told me that this had always been their dream together, that they would retire, sell their home and buy a motor home to cruise down Route 66 in The States. Even in the spirit world, even without his wife, the spirit was still able to live out his dream and his life, in a way, continued. As he told me to say, he was checking out all the tourist stops, ready for when his wife joined him. This is what I try to help my students understand and incorporate into their readings.

Though I return to certain methods and lessons, I try to tailor my courses to the person I'm teaching and what they are there to learn. One of my courses is simplifying mediumship, critiquing students, and beginning afresh. At the same time, I'm trying to teach each individual separately. As with learning other skills, people learn and develop mediumship in different ways. And I have to try and cater for those 20 to 30 different ways.

During my courses and circles, I try not to throw students into the deep end. I have developed and continue to use a variety of approaches to help mediums build their connection with Spirit. One of the exercises I use for beginners only needs paper and a flipchart. I will draw a shape or simple image on the flipchart that they can't see. Then I ask students to attempt to intuit, to ask Spirit, what the image is and draw it on their paper. By getting them to draw it, their answers are set in stone, there are no attempts to 'cheat'. If I reveal that I've drawn a tree and they have too, then we have to ask where did that come from? While this sharpens the skills they will use as a medium, it is also a trust exercise between them and Spirit. By using these small stakes, students can gain that belief and assurance that yes, Spirit is there and can communicate with you, in one way or another.

One of my favourite exercises is geared more towards very new mediums. The purpose is to help students sharpen their clairsentience, being able to sense Spirit before hearing or seeing. Again, this begins with a piece of paper. See, no need for £100 crystal balls or 100-year-old tarot cards that you bid for on eBay. It is very low cost. To start, I have students scan their bodies, noting any aches, pains, sensations and emotions. I tell them that anything they currently feel is theirs. This way, they become fully tuned with themselves and what is of and from them.

I ask them to invite Spirit, saying they are ready to work and then step onto the paper. They can build that connection with Spirit and begin to communicate for an audience member or student. Having a physical medium to begin with helps make that self/Spirit distinction clear, and helps them recognise that mentally. When they can do this, I ask them to step back and off the paper, maintaining that connection and understanding what is coming from Spirit. It's like taking the stabilisers off their bikes. Some of them will wobble and fall, lose that connection with Spirit, but as soon as I ask them to step back on the paper, they're back in action. They'll feel pulled this way or that, with their hearts racing.

Starting with these exercises helps students become aware of Spirit, the crucial first step. They need to acknowledge what is around them, what they're going into, before attempting any kind of communication. Feelings such as light-headedness or heart racing, emotions like depression or anger, they're able to understand they're from Spirit, then linking those sensations to an individual spirit. From there, the connection builds.

I still use this technique, even with already working mediums. Some of them have only ever used thought processes and internal methods. Introducing something more tangible becomes an entryway into picking up on things they had not or could not before. A student steps on the paper and begins to scratch their leg. Without that physical part, you might not recognise that it's coming from Spirit and ignore it. However, acknowledging that while on the paper the sensations are coming from Spirit, you recognise this and you can connect the leg scratching with the spirit being an amputee.

Before anyone tries it, there is no cheating in mediumship lessons. There's no glancing at your neighbour's test or saying yes, you also see the spirit of Henry VIII. Because I will know. If a student is communicating with a spirit, it isn't a closed conversation. It's all coming from the same source, so I would be able to tap in too. It's like old landline phones, one upstairs and one downstairs, and if someone calls, multiple people can chime in.

Another medium, Josephine, is able to draw the spirit that I am communicating with. As a tutor, it's been an invaluable teaching skill. If a student is stuck on an image or a piece of information, I can help them understand or reinterpret it. For example, they might not understand a name they're given as the name of a person. If I come in, I can see that it's not a person's name, but a street name. Highlighting these differences and collaborating on what Spirit is giving us helps sharpen each student's skills.

As with any teaching endeavour, there is more than just the curriculum, there's debunking preconceived ideas, reassuring that it will be fine, and hand-holding if it all goes wrong. Teaching mediumship is no different. Students will need to be told explicitly, and sometimes several times, that no, spirits are not going to follow you home; no, just because that last spirit you spoke to had a stroke doesn't mean you're going to.

Fair enough that they need a bit of understanding. It is not the same level of debunking as when random audience members are frightened that their recently departed grandparent is going to start harassing them in the shower. These students are working closely with spirits and the spirit world. They want to double-check the potential occupational hazards. And because they are dealing with the public, sometimes on a large scale, there is always the anxiety of getting it wrong.

'Your dad isn't in Spirit? Oh, he's sitting next to you… Hi Dad…'

Every medium has the same fear when first demonstrating. Doing it in circle when you're all learning or conducting one-on-one readings is very different from a room full of strangers. If you get it wrong, you get it wrong. We just go back to the spirit and check, was something missed? Was something misinterpreted? Can you clarify that for me? Spirit isn't there to catch mediums out. If something was misunderstood, we can check, maybe there is another way to be shown the message or understand it.

Some people just need to be told, 'Yes, you can do it. I believe in you.' Not everyone is lucky enough to have that from friends and family. When I was first developing my gifts, I kept it all to myself. I didn't want anyone to think I was crazy.

There are times when students will step up to the platform, try to connect with Spirit and draw a blank. The greatest chef will have dishes that don't quite work. The greatest writers will have writer's block. Getting these blanks happens. From a medium's point of view, it's about understanding why it happens, and what's going on with the medium. A lot of the time, it's students coming away from Spirit and going into their own minds. When students are doing well and it seems that one day, they're getting nothing, I have to assure them that Spirit is not abandoning them. More often than not, there is a bigger picture: something going on that is more important than communicating with Spirit, something they need to focus on.

Watching and teaching and experiencing these budding mediums was, and continues to be such an experience. Their confidence grows, their skills expand, and their gifts continue to improve. Conducting readings and demonstrations, you get used to that instant validation. The boost to your confidence, your faith, never diminishes, but it becomes part of the package. With teaching, however, I learned to appreciate the slow burn of success and validation. Weeks and months we would spend together, going through trial and error. Then one day it clicks, and it brings me great joy knowing I am the one guiding them, that everything that I have learned is helping others.

Debbie's Story

While Arlene's story ticked all the boxes of a natural predisposition to mediumship, Debbie's story did that and more.

***

Though I'd never fully explored it and had never looked into churches or centres, I'd always had an interest in spiritualism. After an intense experience in a mortuary, this interest became something more.

While waiting for major surgery, I sadly lost my younger brother, Paul. I was asked to come and identify the body at the mortuary. I confirmed that it was my brother and then I became aware of Paul standing beside me. Unbelievable, he couldn't have been clearer, I was assured that his voice wasn't in my head. Classic Paul, he said that if he could get up off the table, he'd have said boo!

He said how sorry he was, but quickly turned to more important matters, that his hair hadn't been gelled and it was too long. There was no denying it now, I thought. Not only was there a life after death, but Paul was still living in some way, and I had been able to hear him.

That might've been enough to convince me to explore this path, my gift. But clearly, Spirit wanted to give me an extra push. During a visit to my grandma's with a cousin, I became aware that my cousin was dealing with some difficulty. No one had told me this, not even him. All I could say was that somehow, I knew. I tried to reassure him, that if there was something wrong, there were people he could talk to. Only weeks later, he tried to take his life.

No denying it, no ignoring it, I was desperate to find some help. And unfortunately, 'Help, I can hear the dead now,' yields few helpful links on Google.

Talking to myself in the car as I usually do, trying to figure out what to do next and where to go, I dropped my phone. When I looked at it again, it was unlocked and showed an advert for 'The Voice of Spirit'. I'd never heard of the place, but as it happened, there was a meeting that very night. You can shout coincidence all you like, but I wouldn't agree. This was a sign and there was no way I could not go.

I called my son and asked if he'd come to see 'the spooks' with me. Though he agreed at first, he insisted that his girlfriend's mother, Janice, might be better company. During the meeting, Dominic connected to Paul and was able to pass messages to me, both on the circumstances and the cause of his death. Right down to his gestures, there was no question that Dominic was talking to Paul.

Dom told me that a woman had tried to revive Paul, but it was already too late. He told me what Paul showed him: Paul being pulled off the couch, this woman trying to revive him. He'd lost a trainer and, as Dom said, he was gutted that his 'good' t-shirt had been cut. More and more details, things only the immediate family knew. Paul was even able to tell me that the lost trainer was stuck down the side of the sofa. When I was able to check, there it was. Not only that but when my mum received Paul's belongings, there was the cut-up t-shirt.

Convinced beyond belief, I was eager to attend my development circle. As nervous and even intimated as I felt, according to Dom, I was a natural, guided by Spirit from the off. While other students gave readings to each other, Dom asked me to stand behind a whiteboard and write whatever came to mind, or rather, whatever words and details Spirit gave me. Panicking, I realised I wasn't getting anything – no words, no feelings, hints or senses. Eventually, I managed to calm down and filter out the voices in the room. Soon, I was able to see the words in my head. Dom reminded me to write or draw anything I saw, exactly as given, no matter how bizarre or random. When revealed, I had received and written every word accurately. I was shocked.

Within a matter of weeks, Dom had me up performing; even if he had to trick me a little first. He'd invited me to watch him, but in the last minutes, he told me I was the one demonstrating. Doing it all in class was one thing, but in front of a full audience, I gathered my courage and my faith and went for it. I like to think I held my own and Dom seemed happy.

***

Truth be told, Debbie needed very little instruction from me. She was a natural, giving 100% of herself to Spirit. A real protégé and a testament to her talents, I continue to be so proud of Debbie and bowled over by her accomplishments.

Epilogue
Then There Was COVID

I do not need to remind anyone of what happened in March 2020. No one is going to forget anytime soon. COVID came and the country went into lockdown. I won't be the first or last to admit that it was a scary and strange time. No one knew what was really happening, or what was going to happen. All of our lives slowed to a grinding halt.

And before anyone asks, no I did not know COVID was coming. I think it's clear by now that I am not in the business of predicting and prophesying, I am no Nostradamus. If you don't know that, I would consider a reread. But I do remember that many private psychic readings leading up to the lockdown had taken a negative turn. I was telling people about losing their homes or losing their jobs. Loss and disruption were the repeated themes, but the sitter would be able to pick up the pieces.

At the time, I didn't think much of it, I rarely do; after all, it's not my reading. Once lockdown began, I began to reflect on all those readings. It wasn't just me. People I'd read contacted me, asking if I knew this would happen; if when I said they'd lose this or that, I was talking about lockdown? For the record, I did not know there was going to be a pandemic. I don't think anybody could.

Though most of my work is very fast-paced, jumping from private reading to private reading, and living out of a suitcase on tour, I was lucky in a way. Back when I was writing for The Sun, I was already working 'remotely', and had been since. I had been using Zoom and other apps for years. To conduct readings, I didn't need the person there, all I needed was their voice. I am fully aware that this was a luxury not afforded to all people or all mediums. But I have always been one to take any opportunity to work.

Shows were cancelled, refunds processed and private readings moved online. I was getting a peek into people's living rooms as well as connecting with their loved ones. With virtual readings available, my international following began to grow. All these people sitting at home had to do something, why not have a reading with a medium? I was getting requests and bookings from Turkey, Israel, and Singapore to name a few. I had never even been to most of these countries, but here they were, on my computer screen, ready for a reading.

Not only private readings, but more opportunities for teaching arrived on my doorstep. I was creating and running classes, courses and workshops; I had the time after all. One of the classes was for 20 students in Sweden. While most people were on their 100th Zoom quiz, I was still teaching people how to connect with Spirit. I could never have imagined such an experience before COVID.

As lockdown dragged on, spring turning into summer, I was postponing or cancelling more and more shows. We had become accustomed to everything being virtual, from classes to readings, family birthdays and celebrations, but it wasn't until someone gave me the idea, I thought about doing whole streamed events. Why not? People were running entire companies from their dining room tables and students preparing for exams via Zoom. I had no excuse.

Mark and I bought all the necessary accoutrements including a 60-inch screen, and turned our spare bedroom into a studio. It wasn't exactly Lorraine Kelly, but it worked for us. Once we were all set, I was doing a couple of events a week, pages of videos of people asking for messages. Despite the mess of the outside world, people were still searching for healing and messages of reassurance. I was still grateful that I could do that from home.

In the most bizarre of times, Spirit was able to fulfil me, keep me working and helping people. And people needed help and healing, now more than ever before. Shortly into lockdown, I was dealing with people who had lost loved ones during and from COVID. People had not been able to say goodbye to relatives; funeral attendance was kept to a minimum. So, people looked to me as a medium for reassurance, for closure. In a nutshell, my job was and still is to help people through their grief.

Even I needed some time to deal with and process these feelings. Mediums have to take the weight of some of these dark emotions. I know I can have sensations and images that I can't always shake immediately, especially after a particularly tragic reading. Mark and I found the time to take on another personal project. Working in the garden, we managed to build some decking and buy a water feature, creating a little sacred space for me. I say Mark and I, but credit where credit's due, I was not laying any decking. After readings or events, I often found myself out there, going through the motions of dealing with that reading or demonstration. It was especially beautiful during those long summer evenings of 2020, a consolation prize for lockdown, I guess.

Though I had been with Mark for years, we had never really been stuck to each other the way we were during lockdown. It was a chance to be together, to be at home. My neighbour is my mum, so we formed a bubble with her from the very beginning. Our cul-de-sac of five became a little community. We could sit outside and socialise at a distance.

For the first time in a long time, I was at home for more than a few weeks and surrounded by family. Mum was only next door, Mark's family were five minutes away and my grandparents were 10 minutes. Touring as much as I had, I had missed my fair share of birthdays and anniversaries and other family events. This worldwide pause meant I could catch up, appreciate my family and be at home.

Everything was thrown into perspective, from our jobs to our families, our friends to our health, everything about our lives became precarious. Finally, we were starting to understand that and starting to be grateful for what we had. We were all reassessing what our lives meant.

Yes, I loved the travelling part of my job, connecting with every kind of person imaginable. But Port Glasgow has always been my home. My roots there go deep; no matter how far away I am, no matter how amazing a time I've had, I'm always happy to go back home. When my job didn't stop, neither did I. Having a home and roots and a family was something I took for granted. I don't think I appreciated it as much until lockdown.

I do count myself lucky and I fully acknowledge that wasn't the case for everyone. But I had the chance to slow down, to take stock of my life and everything I was grateful for. For once, I wasn't stuck in some hotel room or having dinner at some service station. The lockdown was far from ideal, but I was able to take a breather.

This is why I wanted to write this memoir, to memorialise my life so far. By putting pen to paper, figuratively at least, I was able to take stock of what has made my life great. The people, the places and the experiences have all been thanked in these pages.

And what does the future hold? Who knows? But I have plans. During lockdown, I had the time to think and meditate on what I wanted to do next with my mediumship, and where I wanted to take it. I still felt passionate about teaching, nurturing developing mediums and helping established mediums improve.

But just as everybody sacrificed a lot for our own and everyone's safety, so these students sacrificed their development.

As we came out of lockdown, as the country and the world began to open up again, I could sense this want for teaching. For developing mediums, they might have begun their training before COVID. Due to lockdown, they didn't have the chance to continue. Their gifts and their interest might have plateaued. For established mediums, just as they were finding new ways, they had to stop. Rather than plateauing, they probably felt a bit stagnant, cut off from their peers and mentors. Let's not forget anyone who began to have an inkling, an awakening or spiritual moment, and had no accessible community to help them. I couldn't wait to get stuck back in and teach.

Of course, I went straight ahead and jumped in at the deep end. The first order of business was a residential teaching seminar. I love hosting and being part of these days, or week-long residential experiences. This is where 'Together With Spirit' was born. As my accomplices, I had Josephine MacKenzie, a spirit artist and wonderful medium, and Scott Milligan, a trance and physical medium. Together, we would host classes, seminars and workshops, dedicated to all things spiritual and mediumship, offering whatever guidance we could.

We decided to base the residential in a manor house in the heart of Scotland. Students flew in from all over to attend: Sweden, Holland, England, Belgium. Clearly, we were right and there was a desire for this kind of gathering. Thankfully, it was a success, so much so, that we hosted the residential another three times in Scotland.

In 2023, I am going to host a residential in The Netherlands, this time named 'Walking with The Unseen'. Again, Scott and Josephine will be by my side. Always one to go bigger and bigger, I am excited to soon plan and hold residentials in more countries including the US.

Talking of the States, there are bountiful opportunities still waiting for me there. On every trip, I seem to make another connection, meet another medium, and somehow book myself into another church in another state. This year will be a year of firsts: first time to Canada, to Colorado, to Miami. Maybe I'll get the chance to explore other passions like inspirational speaking. I've never been shy about my love of talking, and I'll talk to anyone. But I'm excited to talk to whole audiences, the public, about mediumship and delivering messages of hope. Each opportunity that lands on my doorstep, I will continue to accept with open and grateful hands.

More teaching, more travelling and more readings and shows means more writing fodder. I always intended for this book to be one of many, or at least a few. In the future, I plan on creating a mediumship teaching manual, my methodology and lessons reaching even further afield. But there will be more adventures and will need penning too. Later in 2023, I will be taking *The Voice of Spirit* on a book tour, making connections and showing people that life is eternal. I'm bound to pick up more stories along the way. You'll have to wait for the next book to read all about them.

Acknowledgements

There are countless people to whom I owe enormous thanks, not only for supporting me in the writing of this memoir but supporting me along this strange and wonderful path.

I could never imagine achieving a fraction of what I have achieved without my partner, Mark. He gave up his dream for me, to manage me, ground me and build new dreams with me. He was never going to let my ego get out of control. The best manager and chauffeur I could ask for.

Thank you to my mum, Rita, who has never stopped me from being anything other than myself. She believed in me from the very beginning; from driving me to my first private readings, and for the cheeky McDonald's afterwards, to supporting my development. She has done nothing but love me and nurture me. I am the gentleman I am because she showed me how.

To my Gran and Grandad, Alec and Margaret Hellyer, they were my strength and foundation from which I grew. Even when the world was dark and difficult, they always brought me back, reminding me of all that is beautiful in the world.

To my brother and sister, Stuart and Danielle; when the world could've called me crazy, they had my back. My greatest cheerleaders, they have kept me, their brother who speaks to the dead, in line, not always an easy task.

To Mark's mum, Elizabeth, my right-hand lady. She helped create the perfect space at The Voice of Spirit Centre. Late nights cleaning or making teas and sandwiches, my little helper always.

To Sandra Bell, there are many things I need to thank her for, and I don't know where to begin. For starters, she was the voice of my father, connecting with Mum and me, ultimately bringing me under her wing. She recognised the light in me, pushed me to be the best medium I could be, and gave me so many opportunities.

To Nick Kyle and Sarah Grumpbell, without whom this book would still be just an idea. From The Voice of Spirit, they encouraged me throughout this book's creation. Nick has given so much of his time, urging me to write it all down. He said that just because I couldn't see the book, didn't mean it couldn't become a reality; he made it a reality. They conducted interviews, researched my life, and set up experiments that make up the material of my memoir.

To my best pal, Siobhan, who has been with me through all the tears and tantrums of being a medium. She has always steered me back to who I am and why I do this work. Together, we've had endless journeys to demonstrations and private readings, often getting lost, no thanks to the satnav. She has endured several strange and crazy parties where I've done private readings. I couldn't have asked for a better supporter.

This book would be only a couple of pages long if not for the generous people who have allowed me to share their stories. An extra special thank you to Arlene, Ross, Debbie and Lynn for accompanying me on this journey, and for helping me with the painting at The Voice of Spirit. We are a part of each other's lives forever.

To Gemma Purdy for my photoshoot and the front cover picture. Thank you for being patient with me.

Thank you to one very special lady, Mary DiGiovanni. I came into her life for only a week, back when I was a very naïve young man during my first time in America. Ten years on, we are family. The opportunities she gave me, my launch in America that she devised, I am blessed to have her in my family.

To those I worked with at The Scottish Sun, Anna, Lynn and Yvonne, I am so grateful for the chance they gave me, to write my own column, the chance to grow my platform and my connections to people who needed me. It was, and remains, a very special part of my life. I am so lucky that you had faith in me.

Thank you to my assistant, Kimberley, she of unbounded patience. She has been my eyes, dealing with endless emails day in and day out. She has been and played a huge part in this book coming together.

And lastly but most importantly, a thank you to James Reynolds, the man behind the words of this book. He took the manuscript and the research, and transformed them into my story, with my voice. Your endless patience and your crazy questions, all to get the most from me, have made this book what it is. It has been a pleasure to work with you and I'm so thankful for your part in creating my dream. To say that this book would not be possible without you would be an understatement. I look forward to our journeys to come.

Available worldwide from Amazon

www.mtp.agency

mtp.agency

@mtp_agency

Made in the USA
Middletown, DE
26 March 2024